Advance praise

"*Amazing Graces* is a fascinating and unique look at the sacramentals of the Catholic Church. Author Julie Dortch Cragon tells engaging stories about each sacramental as she explains how these beneficial channels of grace can give you a tangible sense of God in your life."
—Donna-Marie Cooper O'Boyle, EWTN TV host
and author of *The Miraculous Medal*

"What treasures lie within our reach! Julie Dortch Cragon unveils the sometimes unknown—and too often misunderstood—richness of Catholic sacramentals. Through her historical, spiritual, and personal insights, we discover anew the wealth of graces available to us. This book is a blessing in itself.
—Gina Loehr, author, *Saint Francis, Pope Francis*

"In *Amazing Graces: The Blessings of Sacramentals*, Julie Dortch Cragon gifts us with a serious and challenging consideration of the role of sacramentals in our Church and in our prayer lives. Far from simply just 'decorations' or feel-good traditions, these powerful tools give us the profound opportunity to know, share, and truly love our Catholic faith. This book belongs in every Catholic home."
—Lisa M. Hendey, author, *The Grace of Yes*

"This book warmed my heart and reminded me why I love being Catholic!"
—Jon M. Sweeney, author, *The Pope Who Quit* and
When Saint Francis Saved the Church

"*Amazing Graces* is a much-needed book, as sacramentals are so often misunderstood and undervalued in our Catholic culture today. My gratitude to Julie Dortch Cragon for bringing this vital part of our faith back to life."

—Marge Fenelon, author, *Strengthening Your Family* and *Imitating Mary*

"Along with the usual suspects—a rosary, holy water—Julie Dortch Cragon rounds up the objects, prayers, and activities God uses as a delivery system for his grace. As she explains fasting, nativity scenes, and more, we are encouraged to grow closer to Christ through the concrete gifts of this world."

—Karen Edmisten, author, *After Miscarriage*

"In *Amazing Graces* Julie Dortch Cragon outlines the small, everyday things we can do to nurture our soul and helps us understand all the graces that surround us in the Catholic Church."

—Brian Kennelly, author, *Two Statues* and *To the Heights: A Novel Based on the Life of Pier Giorgio Frassati*

"In this inspiring and informative book, Julie Dortch Cragon shows how sacramentals are amazing graces that draw us nearer to God and bear witness to his presence in our world. She highlights many traditional prayers, objects, and practices that make the moments of our life holy."

—Bert Ghezzi, author, *Living the Sacraments* and *The Heart of Catholicism*

AMAZING GRACES

Amazing Graces

The Blessings of Sacramentals

JULIE DORTCH CRAGON

servant

AN IMPRINT OF
FRANCISCAN MEDIA
Cincinnati, Ohio

LIBRARY OF CONGRESS CONTROL NUMBER: 2015932429

ISBN 978-1-61636-872-2

Published by Servant, an imprint of Franciscan Media
28 W. Liberty St.
Cincinnati, OH 45202
www.FranciscanMedia.org

Printed in the United States of America.
Printed on acid-free paper.
15 16 17 18 19   5 4 3 2 1

::: CONTENTS :::

::: INTRODUCTION :::

Sacramentals are sacred signs instituted by the Church. They prepare men to receive the fruit of the sacraments and to sanctify different circumstances of life.

—*Catechism of the Catholic Church*, 1677

Being Catholic is more than just going to Mass once a week and receiving the sacraments. Being Catholic is a way of life. In practicing our faith, we are constantly looking for ways to spend time with God, asking for help from his mother and the saints. Sacramentals are items, actions, and blessings that remind us to be faithful, to pray, to love one another, and to be grateful to our God, who is merciful and who loves us unconditionally. They move us to think about our faith, about our Catholic way of life, and most importantly, about God.

Of premier importance among sacramentals are "*blessings* (of persons, meals, objects, and places)," the *Catechism* tells us. "[T]he Church imparts blessings by invoking the name of Jesus, usually while making the holy sign of the cross of Christ" (*CCC* 1671; emphasis in original). In addition, "The religious sense of the Christian people has always found expression in various forms of piety surrounding the Church's sacramental life, such as the veneration of relics, visits to sanctuaries, pilgrimages, processions, the stations of the cross, ... the rosary, medals, etc." (*CCC* 1674).

The Church gives us sacramentals, whereas Christ himself instituted the sacraments. Sacramentals help draw us closer to Christ. With prayer and with the proper intention, the many beautiful sacramentals help us focus on that which is holy and make holy many occasions of our lives. Although we do not need them for salvation, sacramentals draw us into deeper devotion and prayer.

As I entered the home of my friends John and Kim Derrick several months ago, I noticed the framed sketch of a Dominican sister hanging in the living room, the oversized rosary beads on the end table, and the crucifix on the wall. Kim had heard that children's eyes are drawn toward the sacred and the beautiful, and she wants Jesus and the example of religious vocation and prayer to be a part of her family. She wants the beautiful images of our Church to be familiar to her children and the use of the rosary, holy water, and scapulars to bless their everyday lives.

I believe we are in a time when we need every bit of help we can find to keep our children and ourselves on track in living a truly authentic Catholic life, our eyes and thus our minds focused on the sacred. Sacramentals are spiritual tools that we must pass on to the next generations. Our grandparents and parents gave many of us good examples in praying the rosary, saying novenas, and having statues and images of the saints, Mary, and Jesus in the house. These reminders helped keep them focused on what was important: faith and trust in God. Sacramentals continue to help Catholics today.

In 1984, I backpacked through Europe. After traveling through parts of the Netherlands, Germany, Switzerland, Italy, and Greece with a friend, I headed for the south of France. Landing in Lourdes, I stayed with a group of seminarians from Ireland in a house run by a nun and her brother.

I tried to make the most of the few days I had to visit the grotto where the Blessed Mother appeared to St. Bernadette. The first day I went to Mass and confession and prayed before the life-size Stations of the Cross. I washed my face with the water from the spouts tapped into the side of the hill and lit candles for everyone I could think of. That night, I stood on top of the basilica and prayed the rosary with thousands of other people, all in our own languages. Thousands also walked in procession with the sick and the suffering—some in wheel-chairs or with walkers—carrying candles, lifting prayers to Our Lady. I was deeply moved in my heart and in my soul.

This moment changed my life. I longed to be closer to Our Lady and to allow her to bring me closer to her son. The sacramentals at the shrine—the rosary, the Stations of the Cross, the candles, and the Lourdes water—all played a huge part in bringing me back to the example of my parents and grandparents.

I would return to Lourdes many years later, pregnant with my fifth child. At that point I realized the importance of my commitment to these sacramentals as witness for my family. Every day, I work on that commitment.

Pope Francis, in his address from St. Peter's Square on May 18, 2013, said, "Today's world stands in great need of witnesses, not so much of teachers but rather of witnesses. It's not so much about speaking, but rather speaking with our whole lives."[1]

We, as Catholics, are fortunate to have a faith that is rich in tradition. Part of this is sacramentals, which have been passed down through the Church for centuries. The rewards and promises of joy associated with their use are for us today. As we use sacramentals to enhance our Catholic way of life—as we bless ourselves, genuflect, pray the rosary, and so on—may we be witnesses to the love of God and help others to be the same.

::: CHAPTER ONE :::

The Sign of the Cross

> At every forward step and movement, at every going in and
> out, when we put on our clothes and shoes, when we bathe,
> when we sit at table, when we light the lamps...in all the ordi-
> nary actions of daily life, we trace upon the forehead the sign.[2]
> —TERTULLIAN, *DE CORONA*

Let us begin as we begin all prayer: In the name of the Father, and of
the Son, and of the Holy Spirit. Amen.

The Sign of the Cross is the sacramental most frequently used by
Catholics. Many of the earliest references to it are in the writings of
the Church fathers. Tertullian, Origen, St. John Chrysostom, St. Cyril
of Jerusalem, and St. Augustine speak of frequent and reverent signing
with the cross—when Christians rise in the morning, before and after
their meals, as they pass through doorways, and as they work. Learning
of the symbolism and the importance of the gesture from past scholars
has made what seems to be a natural motion—as I genuflect, or dip my
hand in holy water, or begin Mass—increase in value and importance.
Suddenly, the Sign of the Cross is a complete prayer within itself.

So important is this blessing that many explanations have been
offered as to how to hold our hands and fingers as we make the Sign of
the Cross. Early Christians made the Sign of the Cross on their foreheads with the thumb, just as is done today in the sacraments of baptism
and confirmation and in the distribution of ashes on Ash Wednesday.
We more often bless ourselves with the "large" Sign of the Cross—
touching the forehead, the chest, and each shoulder. Most of us use the
open hand, representing the five wounds of Christ. Following earlier

teachings, some people hold down the baby finger and ring finger with the thumb and cross themselves with two fingers, symbolizing the two natures of Jesus, human and divine.

A third popular form is to touch the tip of the thumb to the tips of the first two fingers, using these three fingers to symbolize the Trinity. Meanwhile, the baby finger and ring finger bend down into the palm, again representing the humanity and the divinity of Jesus. This final form is similar to how a priest or bishop holds his hand while giving a blessing. The instruction explains that the two small fingers are bent slightly, with the upper finger representing Jesus's divinity and the lower his humanity, noting that he came down from heaven for our salvation.

Regardless of how we hold our fingers, the Sign of the Cross reminds us of all that God has done for us. The cross is love poured out for us. God the Father gave us his Son, "not to condemn the world, but that the world might be saved through him" (John 3:17, RSV). There is no greater sign of love than the cross.

There are many times we bless ourselves with the Sign of the Cross. Upon entering a church, we generally dip our hands into the holy water font and make the Sign of the Cross. Many people make the Sign of the Cross when genuflecting before entering the pew, in honor of Jesus in the tabernacle.

There are also many occasions when the priest or bishop blesses us with the Sign of the Cross. Mass begins and ends with the Sign of the Cross. If a deacon reads the Gospel, the priest makes the Sign of the Cross over him, asking God to be in his heart and on his lips, that he may proclaim the Word worthily. Before the Gospel reading, the priest or deacon traces the Sign of the Cross on the Book of the Gospel. Then he traces the cross on his forehead, lips, and heart. The congregation does the same. We pray that we may allow the message into our minds, speak the message from our mouths, and bear the message in our hearts. We are all called to believe and to preach and to love the teachings of Christ.

The priest makes the Sign of the Cross over the bread and the wine as he prepares them for consecration. Toward the end of Mass, a pastor might have extraordinary ministers come forth and receive a special blessing before going to distribute Communion to the sick and homebound.

We all are blessed with the Sign of the Cross as we receive the sacraments, whether the small cross traced on our foreheads with oil at baptism and confirmation or the large blessing bestowed by a priest or a deacon at the end of each Mass. Within the Church, we are constantly reminded of the cross. It is a sign of the Trinity, of Christ's love for us, and of his request that we go and be signs of that cross ourselves as we live the Christian life.

Christ does not want this blessing to end as we leave the Church. In our homes too, as we bless our meals, as we say our morning and night prayers, we make the Sign of the Cross. Many of the Church fathers preached that we should sign everything. St. Cyril of Jerusalem wrote, "Let us not be ashamed to confess the Crucified. Let the cross, as our seal, be boldly made with our fingers upon our brow and on all occasions; over the bread we eat, over the cups we drink, in our comings and in our goings; before sleep; on lying down and rising up; when we are on the way and when we are still."[3]

Many of us are taught to make the sign of the cross as we drive past a church, reminding us of the presence of Jesus in the Tabernacle, or when we hear the siren of an ambulance, praying for the person in distress.

What a wonderful habit it is to make the Sign of the Cross frequently, to bring Christ to our minds and to our hearts as we carry the crosses of life on our shoulders and bear witness to him in our work and in our homes, as we travel and as we rest, in our encounters with others! With this sign, we participate in the mystery of the Trinity and are reminded that from the Father came the Son, and from them, the Holy Spirit, who gives us the strength and the knowledge to bear witness to the truth.

::: **WITNESS** :::

One night, while working with my daughter on her First Communion journal, I was moved by her ideas about prayer. The first page of the journal asked her to take time in prayer and just talk to God about her day, about her life, and about her upcoming First Communion. She suddenly said, "Mom, you know when we go during school into the church, and we pray in front of Jesus, when there is that huge gold thing, you know?"

"The monstrance, during Eucharistic Adoration?"

"Yes. When we first get there and kneel down, and I do this." She made the Sign of the Cross and said slowly, "In the name of the Father and of the Son and of the Holy Spirit."

"Yes?"

"I pretend that that," she crossed herself again, "is like knocking on God's door, and I wait for him to let me in. Then, when I'm inside, I see him in one of those shade hats [a visor], and he's at one of those old machines that you move your fingers to type and then push the bar back [a typewriter], and there are stacks of white paper all over around him, like with what people ask for and prayers and stuff, and I just wait to talk to him."

So we went to pray, and she said, "Make sure to knock on the door each time." We slowly made the Sign of the Cross, as she knelt in silence. Then she sat down and wrote in her journal, "I want you to speak to me. I want you to speak to me. Amen."

I watched her, knowing how much Jesus loved this moment: my second-grader explaining the importance of beginning my prayers with the Sign of the Cross. I will wait for Jesus to open the door to my prayers of desire and of thanksgiving, which he has already in the stacks of white paper all over his desk. He loves to have me come to him over and over, and he answers no matter how often I knock.

My daughter expressed frustration at the fact that she cannot hear him speak.

"He sometimes answers us by action or in silence," I said, "and sometimes not as soon as we ask. Keep knocking on that door, and take time to just be quiet and listen." I said these words for myself as well.

Suddenly, my daughter was fine. She hopped up and said, "You know, I think Jesus would like it if you wrote a prayer to him on your blog." Then she was off to brush her teeth.

Often, from the teaching of God's little ones, we learn the simplest means of reaching him. We learn to be like little children, to knock on the door and come to him. When we listen with our hearts, we will hear the answers he gives for all our needs.

Jesus opens the door. Through his sacraments and through the sacramentals the Church gives us, we can honor and love him, which leads us to honor and love one another.

I will write a prayer. But before I begin, I will knock.

::: GRACE :::

I typically say to myself before the reading of the Gospel at Mass, as I trace the cross on my head and my lips and my heart, "May the Gospel stay in my mind, on my lips, and in my heart, that I may go out and proclaim his words to those I come in contact with throughout the day." But I have never put much thought into a quick Sign of the Cross over myself. Now I am drawn to pray, "May I do all in the name of the Father and of the Son and of the Holy Spirit. Let this cross be a reminder of God's complete love for me."

Jesus died on this cross so that we may someday be with him in heaven. We are empowered by the cross to live his words, to imitate his life, to love beyond all understanding. This Sign of the Cross is so much more than a gesture to begin and end a prayer. This sign truly leads us to the Lord, because the cross is our faith and our redemption. The cross teaches truth.

::: **PRAYER** :::

The Lord is our God, the Lord alone. You shall love the Lord your God with all your heart, and with all your soul, and with all your might. Keep these words that I am commanding you today in your heart. Recite them to your children and talk about them when you are at home and when you are away, when you lie down and when you rise. Bind them as a sign on your hand, fix them as an emblem on your forehead, and write them on the doorposts of your house and on your gates. (Deuteronomy 6:4–9)

In the name of the Father, use my mind to bring you honor, and of the Son, fill my heart to spread your word, and of the Holy Spirit, strengthen me to carry you out to all the world. Amen.

::: **CHALLENGE** :::

Slow down as you make the Sign of the Cross. Intentionally purify your mind and your heart, and ask God to strengthen you to carry his love to the world.

Add one act of the Sign of the Cross to your day, either as you rise from sleep, as you leave the house, or before you go to sleep.

::: CHAPTER TWO :::

The Advent Wreath

When the Church celebrates *the liturgy of Advent* each year,
she makes present this ancient expectancy of the Messiah,
for by sharing in the long preparation for the Savior's first
coming, the faithful renew their ardent desire for his second
coming. By celebrating the precursor's birth and martyrdom,
the Church unites herself to his desire: "He must increase, but
I must decrease."

> —CATECHISM OF THE CATHOLIC CHURCH, 524 (emphasis in
> original; also see Revelation 22:17; John 3:30)

The Church year begins with the first Sunday of Advent. During this
four-week season, we wait in great expectation to celebrate the birth
of Jesus and look forward to his second coming. The Advent wreath is
a popular sacramental that feeds our devotion to the Lord during this
season.

As with many of the older customs of the Church, not much is
known about the history of the Advent wreath. Most people agree
that a wreath similar to what we use today originated in the sixteenth
century in Germany, among the Lutherans. The tradition was brought
to America with the German immigrants and became popular in the
Catholic faith around the 1920s.

The Advent wreath is a symbol of the Light overcoming spiritual
darkness. As the laurel wreath was symbolic of victory, so the wreath of
evergreens represents the one who is to come and win over death. The
circular shape represents the eternity he secures for us. Many people
use holly in their wreaths to signify the crown of thorns, the red berries
reminding us of the blood that Jesus shed for our salvation.

The three purple candles in the wreath symbolize preparation, penance, and sacrifice. We light the one pink candle on the third Sunday of Advent, called *Gaudete* Sunday, meaning "rejoice." The Entrance Antiphon for this day is "Rejoice in the Lord always; again I will say, Rejoice! ... The Lord is near" (Philippians 4:4–5).[4]

Some people include a white candle in the center of the wreath. This is the Christ candle, to be lit on Christmas Day. The purple and pink candles can be replaced with all white candles and can continue to be lit throughout the Christmas season. The gradual increase of light throughout the Advent season brightens into the Light for the World, our Lord and Savior Jesus Christ.

The Advent wreath in the home calls up many different traditions. Whether we make one from a Styrofoam ring or buy one that matches our other Christmas decorations, the wreath is meant to bring us to prayer, to lead us to the Light, and to renew our desire for him in our daily lives. Families seem to develop their own ways of gathering together during this hectic time of year, to read and to pray and to light candles. This sacramental reminds us to slow down, to remember why we give one another gifts, to think about whom we are celebrating.

Another favorite family sacramental during the Advent season is the Advent calendar. Also originating in Germany, the cardboard calendars generally have a Christmas scene on the front, with twenty-five cut-out doors that can be opened, one each day from December 1 until Christmas Day. Each door reveals a scene or a Scripture verse or both that lead us through the season to the birth of Jesus.

::: **WITNESS** :::

As I was reading about this sacramental, I came upon a story of a Protestant pastor in Germany, Johann Hinrich Wichern, who devoted his life to helping the poor and the homeless. He opened Rauhes Haus, a social service institution in Hamburg, Germany, dedicated at that time to helping young boys.

Every year around the end of November, the children would begin asking when it would be Christmas Day. Johann made a large wooden ring from a wagon wheel, decorated it, and put within the greenery twenty small red candles and four large white candles, to set Sundays apart.

Some people believe that the wreaths we use today evolved from this large wreath, made to help children understand the time they had to wait for Christmas Day. The story helps us to understand the importance of the visual for both children and adults. We love to see the approach of our hope.

::: GRACE :::

We acknowledge the first day of Advent as the beginning of the liturgical year. It is a wonderful day to consider new promises for a better year. But as I learned more about the Advent wreath, it came to me that this prayerful devotion of lighting candles and saying prayers of expectancy can be for every day. Each day can be a fresh start of a spiritual tradition. Each day can remind us of Jesus, the Light of the World, his joyful birth, his saving mission. Each day we can pray as did St. John the Baptist, Jesus's precursor, "He must increase, but I must decrease" (John 3:30).

::: PRAYER :::

Lord, help me make my life more about you and less about me. May others see you in me—your image and likeness. Teach me ways to increase my time with you, my service to others, and my love for my family, for strangers, and for the poor.

You are the light in the darkness. With each new day, may we be light to one another.

::: **CHALLENGE** :::

At the start of the liturgical year, light the Advent wreath and gather in prayer. Continue to do this every day until the celebration of the birth of Jesus.

If you already do this each Advent, try gathering once a week throughout the year to light a candle and pray for our world.

CHAPTER THREE

Nativity Scenes

While they were there, the time came for her to deliver her
child. And she gave birth to her firstborn son and wrapped
him in bands of cloth, and laid him in a manger, because there
was no place for them in the inn.

—LUKE 2:6–7

Giovanni Bernardone, nicknamed Francesco by his father, was born in
Assisi, Italy, in the twelfth century. When Francesco was old enough,
he worked with his father, a wealthy cloth maker. He lived a rich and
lively lifestyle.

As time went on, however, Francesco changed. He began giving
to the poor and the outcast. He happened into the Chapel of San
Damiano to pray, and there he heard the voice of God asking him to
rebuild the Church. Francesco took these words literally. He recon-
structed the dilapidated chapel, using all he possessed as well as some
of his father's wealth!

Eventually Francesco renounced his inheritance. In 1208, he began
preaching in the streets, wearing a simple hooded tunic with a rope at
the waist. He and several followers became known as the Friars Minor.
Francesco wrote a simple rule for his order and took it to Rome for
approval. Upon his return, his friars began going out in groups to work
and to preach.

St. Francis of Assisi is credited with the first nativity scene. Seeing
the true meaning of Christmas lost in gift giving, Francesco asked his
friend Giovanni Velitta to prepare a place in Greccio to reenact the
birth of Jesus. On Christmas Eve, in 1223, the people throughout

Greccio brought torches to light the scene that Giovanni had prepared. People of the town played the parts of Mary, Joseph, the innkeeper, and the shepherds. The farmers brought their animals to complete the scene.

An image of the Baby Jesus lay between an ox and an ass while Francesco sang the Gospel and preached about the nativity. That reenactment of the nativity helped all who were there to understand that night when Jesus was born. Since that time, Christmas scenes have become popular all over the world. The characters can be real people or statues made of resin, porcelain, wood, papier-mâché, or other materials. We see crèches inside and outside churches, homes, and businesses.

In central Europe, nativity sets include every animal possible as well as children, townspeople, villagers, vendors, and family members. The words "No room in the inn" have been removed, and all are welcome. Blessed are they who come in his name. Blessed are they who welcome the little ones. As we remember, we imitate.

The nativity scene calls to mind what God has done for his people, for all his people. He sent his Son for our salvation. Gather round. Remember. Put aside the business of the season, and emphasize what really matters. Jesus Christ is born today. Alleluia!

::: **WITNESS** *(by Mary Ann)* :::

My tradition with the nativity scene as a sacramental began with a Fontanini set my mother started for my children. My mother was very insightful when it came to the development of young children. She noticed that the beautiful, hand-painted, ceramic pieces of the nativity scene were rearranged every time she passed through the living room. She came to realize that the crèche was a wonderful sacramental that children are drawn to. Their need to touch and rearrange the pieces is an important part of recounting the beautiful story of the birth of Jesus.

My mother instructed me to place the nativity scene on a low table, at the children's eye level. The children received pieces for Christmas, along with the characters' story cards, which told stories of how the characters were touched by the birth of Jesus. Each year the collection grew. This became an endearing tradition in our family.

As a teacher at a Catholic school, I brought my tradition to the school. Third-grade parents donated pieces to a class Fontanini collection, and we wrote the donor child's name on the bottom of each piece. As the years pass, new third-graders are thrilled to notice the names of their siblings and friends on the bottoms of the pieces as they explore and rearrange the scene.

The kings and their camels are placed along the school hallways, against the walls, during the Advent season. No one disturbs them as they travel each day toward the nativity scene. The children look for them, and even the middle school students have been heard commenting about them when the kings are in their hall. On the Feast of the Epiphany, they are added to the nativity scene in the third-grade classroom, the final destination of their long journey.

Parents have started Fontanini nativities for their families, carrying on the tradition that their children have learned at school. Many godparents have started sets for their godchildren at their baptism. There are enough pieces for every occasion.

Every year the buyers at our local Catholic bookstore go on a buying trip. They place orders for nativity sets, specifically for the Fontanini collections and their extra pieces. The year that my son was diagnosed with cancer, a buyer called on their return from the trip and told me that one of the new shepherds for that year was named Paul, my son's name. Needless to say, everyone on my Christmas list received that special shepherd for Christmas.

::: GRACE :::

Many times in our lives, something that we see every year tends to become expected. Through the stories of how people participate in the birth of Jesus, we learn to place ourselves at "eye level" with our Savior. We can participate in the first part of his life. We follow the star, and we are led to watch the honor given by the lowly shepherds, the stately kings, and even the animals. We begin our own walk in the life of the baby Jesus, and we receive the grace to persevere with him on the journey. The grace of the crèche is the realization that this is more than just a scene in a life. It is the grace to pass Jesus our Savior on to the next generation.

::: PRAYER :::

Lord, may we be inspired by the example of St. Francis to bring the birth of the Baby Jesus into our lives. May we understand a little of what Mary and Joseph had to endure that night to bring the gift of joy, the gift of hope, the gift of love into the world.

May we continually thank you for sending your Son to be our Savior. Help us to truly put aside everything that holds us back from joining together with our community, our families, and our friends to celebrate his birth and the salvation he brings to each of us.

::: CHALLENGE :::

Make a nativity scene the focal point of your Christmas celebration.

Leave out a part of or even all of your nativity set year round, as a small reminder of our salvation.

If you still have children at home, allow your nativity set to be touched and held. Let the children enjoy the journey.

::: **CHAPTER FOUR** :::

Eucharistic Adoration

I urge priests, religious and lay people to continue and redouble their efforts to teach the younger generations the meaning and value of Eucharistic adoration and devotion. How will young people be able to know the Lord if they are not introduced to the mystery of his presence? Like the young Samuel, by learning the words of the prayer of the heart, they will be closer to the Lord, who will accompany them in their spiritual and human growth. The Eucharistic Mystery is in fact the "summit of evangelization" for it is the most eminent testimony to Christ's Resurrection.[5]

—POPE JOHN PAUL II

Devotion to our Lord in the Blessed Sacrament has developed throughout the centuries due to the persistence of many of our great saints and leaders. As early as the year A.D. 325, the Eucharist was kept outside of Mass in monasteries and convents. From there the Eucharist could be taken to the sick and the dying. One of the first references to the Blessed Sacrament being "reserved" in a church comes from the biography of St. Basil. In A.D. 379, it is recorded, he would divide the Eucharistic Bread at Mass, consuming one part himself, giving one part to the monks, and putting the third part in a golden dove suspended over the altar.

Near the end of the eleventh century, Pope Gregory VII defended the Real Presence of Jesus in the Eucharist and called for more public acts of Eucharistic Adoration. Processions of the Eucharist and visits to the Blessed Sacrament became more prevalent. Monasteries had windows constructed so that the monks could see the tabernacle from their cells.

In the thirteenth century, Pope Urban instituted the Feast of Corpus Christi, to be celebrated on Thursday or, in the countries where it is not a holy day, on the Sunday following Trinity Sunday. Pope Clement VIII began Forty Hours Devotion in the sixteenth century, and by the eighteenth century, St. Alphonsus Liguori was writing about the importance of visits to the Blessed Sacrament. He prompted people to spend fifteen minutes to a half hour before the Blessed Sacrament each day, for when we visit Jesus in the Eucharist, St. Alphonsus said, we "obtain a more abundant measure of grace."[6]

In the nineteenth century, St. Peter Julian Eymard and Mother Marguerite Guillot started the Servants of the Blessed Sacrament. This international congregation of women contemplatives is dedicated to continuous Eucharistic Adoration.

The Code of Canon Law states,

> It is recommended that in…churches and oratories an annual solemn exposition of the Most Blessed Sacrament be held for an appropriate period of time, even if not continuous, so that the local community more profoundly meditates on and adores the Eucharistic mystery.[7]

Adoration of the Blessed Sacrament will deepen your relationship with Jesus Christ.

::: **WITNESS** :::

Agnes Gonxha Bojaxhiu was born in 1910 in Skopje, Macedonia. As a teen, she joined the Sisters of Loreto and took the name Teresa. She eventually came to work as a missionary sister in India, where she taught in a Catholic school.

While traveling by train to Darjeeling for a retreat, Sr. Teresa heard her call from God to help the poorest of the poor in the streets. In 1948, she left the Sisters of Loreto, received basic medical training, and then ventured out into the streets of Calcutta. In 1949, a group of young women whom she had previously taught joined her, and in the following year the Vatican gave her permission to start the congregation of the Missionary Sisters of Charity. Her congregation grew rapidly. She opened houses in other parts of India and eventually all over the world.

Mother Teresa credited the sisters' time before our Lord in the Blessed Sacrament with their increase in vocations. The hour-long visits each day gave them the grace to fulfill their mission of going out into the streets and serving the poor and the sick. Mother Teresa also believed that, by visiting Jesus in Eucharistic Adoration, we join with others all over the world in praying for the peace and salvation of all the world.

> In 1973, during the General Chapter of our congregation, there was a unanimous cry, "We want daily adoration of the Blessed Sacrament!"
>
> We have much work to do for the poor. Still we have not had to cut back on our work in order to have that hour of adoration. (Often this is the excuse some people give for not having adoration every day.)
>
> I can tell you I have seen a great change in our congregation from the day we started having adoration every day. Our love for Jesus is more intimate. Our love for each other is more understanding. Our love for the poor is more compassionate. And we have twice as many vocations.[8]

::: GRACE :::

Several summers ago, my mother treated my two older daughters and me to a trip to Spain and Portugal. While in Spain, we stayed mainly in Madrid but took several day trips by train, including a trip to the beautiful old city of Toledo. As we crossed a bridge and entered the walled city with narrow streets and cobblestone walkways, we immediately turned to tourist mode, mapping out what we wanted to see and where we wanted to eat.

Little did we know that there would be so much packed into one small city, including beautiful churches, synagogues, mosques, and museums. Much of our time was spent shopping. There were street vendors and shops everywhere we turned (as if the streets were not narrow enough already).

As we walked one particular stretch between tourist sites, I spotted an old beggar sitting against a wall in the midst of all the hustle and bustle of the street. As I approached, I noticed next to him a slim entranceway marked by a cross and covered with a simple leather flap. I walked over and pulled back the flap to find a tiny room with about ten pews and an altar, where the Blessed Sacrament was exposed in a small monstrance. I entered and knelt, not thinking about my traveling partners, shopping, or anything else. The room drew me in, as I guess it had the handful of others with whom I knelt before Christ.

I prayed for a few minutes in the complete silence of the tiny stone room. The kneelers and the benches were well worn, signs that many others had ventured in for visits with our Lord. I wondered if they too were drawn in by the poor man at the door.

There in the midst of the busy street, through a small opening, in this simple room, was Jesus in the Blessed Sacrament. It was for me a grace given by Christ, conducted by the poor.

::: **PRAYER** :::

Jesus, today you remind us to listen to your call, to enter the tiniest openings, to follow you, and to walk the narrow pathways that lead us to you in the most unexpected places and by the most unlikely of people. We ask for courage to travel even constricted roads that lead us to life with you.

Help us join with others all over the world in prayer before your Blessed Sacrament. Jesus, we adore you.

::: **CHALLENGE** :::

Go. Spend time in front of the Blessed Sacrament. Fifteen minutes, an hour.

CHAPTER FIVE

Ashes

Jonah began to go into the city, going a day's walk. And he
cried out, "Forty days more, and Nineveh shall be overthrown!"
And the people of Nineveh believed God; they proclaimed a
fast, and everyone, great and small, put on sackcloth.

When the news reached the king of Nineveh, he rose from
his throne, removed his robe, covered himself with sackcloth,
and sat in ashes.

—JONAH 3:4–6

Ashes, as a sacramental of the Church, remind us of our sins and our
mortality and therefore our need for repentance. The words of Scripture
teach us how and why we are to turn back to God: We change our ways
that we might win the victory of heaven.

The season of Lent begins with Ash Wednesday. Although not a
holy day of obligation, Ash Wednesday is a day set aside by the Church
to remind us that this life will pass away.

You are dust,
    and to dust you shall return. (Genesis 3:19)

The minister says these words, or others like them, as he signs each
person with ashes on Ash Wednesday.

Christian writers of the fourth and fifth centuries tell of public
displays of penance done by sinners for the forty days leading up
to Easter. They received ashes on their heads from the bishop, who
also blessed their hair shirts as the community recited the penitential
psalms. After difficult penances, the sinners returned to the church on
Holy Thursday.

Pope Gregory the Great, around the late sixth or early seventh century, set Wednesday as the day of the beginning of Lent. Ashes were customary for all members of the Church by the tenth century—either on the forehead in the sign of a cross or sprinkled over the head. The ashes were made by burning the palms used the previous year for Palm Sunday.

Today, on Ash Wednesday, the pope leads a penitential procession from the Monastery of St. Anselm to the Basilica of Santa Sabina. Ashes are sprinkled on his head before he turns to distribute ashes to those in the community.

We too are marked with the Sign of the Cross in ashes as an acknowledgement of our sins. We do not have to put on sackcloth and sit in ashes or wear a hair shirt to show our sorrow and our need for forgiveness. As we wear those ashes on our foreheads in our everyday lives, we are recognized as people in repentance for our sins. We are recognized as Christians beginning a long forty days of prayer and fasting. No matter how far we have strayed, no matter how bad our sins, Jesus is always there, accepting us back into his life, reminding us to pray and to repent.

Ash is used to fertilize soil and to repel garden pests. The right amount of ash in the soil helps plants grow. We too need ash in order to grow. We need that reminder that we are not perfect, that we sin and need to reconcile with God before the end of our life.

::: **WITNESS** :::

The story of Jonah's being sent by God to Nineveh to tell the people to repent of their sins—or their city would be destroyed—is a witness to the power of repentance and mercy and forgiveness. Jonah is called by God, and he runs in the opposite direction. (Most people can probably relate to that response, at least once in their lives.) As Jonah tries to make his way to Tarshish instead of Nineveh, God sends a storm upon the sea. After confessing to the men on the ship that he is the probable cause of God's wrath, Jonah tells them to throw him into the sea.

The sailors try everything before pitching Jonah over. When they finally do pitch him into the sea, a whale swallows Jonah. After three days and much prayer, Jonah is spewed ashore, and he obeys God's second request to go to Nineveh and warn the people.

As Jonah walks across the city and announces the horror that is to come, people repent. When the news gets to the king, he too repents—not only putting on sackcloth like everyone else but sitting in ashes and calling for a strict fast. The king knows that by signing himself with the ashes, he is an example to the rest of his people of sorrow and of pain. He is a witness to his kingdom. This humble act, this sacrifice, brings God to have mercy on the entire city.

::: GRACE :::

Outside of Ash Wednesday once a year, I don't think much about ashes. And yet, I am a sinner. We are all sinners; we are human. Jesus Christ wants us to come to him and to receive forgiveness.

The ashes of Ash Wednesday are smeared on our foreheads in the form of a cross. Jesus died on the cross to redeem us. The cross is a reminder of our need for forgiveness, a reminder of our humanity, a reminder of his mercy.

As we gaze upon the cross, we remember all those to whom we should be an example of repentance. Only God can save us. Only God can save cities that are in turmoil. As I read in Scripture about those needing God's mercy, I realize that this is exactly where we are in our world. We need to sit in the ash, to turn to God and pray for our world. God, forgive us.

::: **PRAYER** :::

Lord, we begin each Lenten season with the mark of ashes upon our foreheads. This mark reminds us of our sinfulness, of our mortality, and of our need for repentance. May we witness this reminder to come to you throughout the year. May we remember this cross of ashes.

Thank you for guiding us in the right direction. Thank you for bringing us to our knees for others and for ourselves. Thank you for always welcoming us back when we have strayed.

Today, we pray for our world. Father, in your great mercy, forgive us.

::: **CHALLENGE** :::

Go to an Ash Wednesday service this year. Wear the cross of ashes throughout the day, and recall the sacrifice, the love, and the mercy of Jesus.

Once a month, or maybe even once a week, recall the cross of ashes. Fast and pray for all of us in need of God's mercy, for we are all in need, and we do not know the hour.

CHAPTER SIX

Palms

The disciples went and did as Jesus had directed them; they
brought the donkey and the colt, and put their cloaks on them,
and he sat on them. A very large crowd spread their cloaks on
the road, and others cut branches from the trees and spread
them on the road. The crowds that went ahead of him and
that followed were shouting,

"Hosanna to the Son of David!

Blessed is the one who comes in the name of the Lord!

Hosanna in the highest heaven!"

When he entered Jerusalem, the whole city was in turmoil,
asking, "Who is this?" The crowds were saying, "This is the
prophet Jesus from Nazareth in Galilee."

—MATTHEW 21:6–11

Palm Sunday, the Sunday before Easter, ushers us into Holy Week.
Beginning in the fourth century, the Church reenacted Christ's entrance
into Jerusalem. The faithful of Jerusalem carried palm branches and
processed to the church. As the tradition spread, a blessing of the palms
was added before the faithful processed to the church for the reading
of the Passion.

Palm branches symbolize victory. Holy Week culminates in Jesus's
victory over death. Often, palm branches are shaped into crosses or
braided and kept in the house until the following year. Then they are
gathered and burned to make the ashes for Ash Wednesday.

As I mentioned above, the palms are blessed, so it is good to put
them in a respectful place in the house, maybe behind a crucifix on

the wall or above a doorway. Throughout the year, palms can remind us to pray in thanksgiving for what Jesus has done in order to give us the opportunity to make it to heaven. His triumphal entrance into Jerusalem, with all the people waving palm branches and celebrating his arrival, marks the beginning of our journey toward salvation. Jesus leads. He is the Way.

::: **WITNESS** :::

Preparation for the triumphal entrance of Jesus on Palm Sunday means something a little different when we are in charge of getting the palms to the occasion. For years our Catholic bookstore has provided palms for the churches in our area. We keep records of what churches request so that we can supply them with the information they may need for the subsequent year. Sometimes numbers in congregations change. Almost every year, we have to rush extra palms in for a church that forgot to order or one that ordered too few. Or perhaps we are trying to sell the extra stock that we guessed we would need. Just once I'd like a victory of hitting the mark exactly.

Then again, this time of year is about the victory of Jesus Christ. The Lenten season, Holy Week, the Easter season are all about the living Christ. While we rush around to satisfy the needs of others, to whom do we owe the glory? Whom do we really need to satisfy? Where is the focus?

As we receive the palms, do we fix our eyes on Jesus? As we wave the palm branches and sing, "Hosanna," do we consider the fact that, in just a few days, we will be chanting, "Crucify him"? As we form our palm branches into crosses, do we remember to wash feet, to come to the table, to kiss the cross, to contemplate in silence, and to recognize the one who will save us? This is the call of Holy Week.

::: GRACE :::

Again we have a sacramental that is used once a year during a specific liturgical celebration. However, forming the palm into a cross to hang above a doorway or sliding a piece behind a crucifix extends the use of this reminder to us of the victory of Christ.

Let these palms be signs for our family. As we envision palms welcoming Christ, we too must welcome others. God gives us the grace to be of service to one another in the journey that leads to Christ. This grace, this ability to welcome others and to lead them on a walk with the living Christ, is a gift that extends beyond the day of his entrance into Jerusalem, beyond the week when we gather to mark his passion and death, beyond his death and resurrection. This grace extends through the years, passed down through the generations and carried day in and day out as a sign of his love.

::: PRAYER :::

Lord, as I gaze upon this blessed palm, may I recall your arrival in the city of Jerusalem. May I welcome you and all in your name.

You have marked the path I should follow. Teach me your ways of service and of love, and bless me with strength for the journey.

::: CHALLENGE :::

Display your blessed palms in your home for all to see. Every month, lay your hand over them and pray for the strength to serve others. Pray for the desire to do God's will in all things.

CHAPTER SEVEN

Incense

> When the Lamb opened the seventh seal, there was silence in
> heaven for about half an hour. And I saw the seven angels who
> stand before God, and seven trumpets were given to them.
>
> Another angel with a golden censer came and stood at the
> altar; he was given a great quantity of incense to offer with the
> prayers of all the saints on the golden altar that is before the
> throne. And the smoke of the incense, with the prayers of the
> saints, rose before God from the hand of the angel.
>
> —REVELATION 8:1–4

Incense symbolizes our offering to God. Just as the smoke rises, so our
prayers rise to heaven.

The use of incense within the liturgy started around the fifth century,
but we read about the use of incense for purification and for veneration
in Scripture. God instructed Moses to make the "plates and dishes for
incense" and then to make an "altar on which to offer incense." Aaron
was to burn incense twice a day, in the morning and the evening, "a
regular incense offering before the Lord" (Exodus 25:29; 30:1, 7–8).

"Let my prayer be counted as incense before you," David prayed
(Psalm 141:2). And so Revelation shows an angel offering incense
with the saints' prayers. "And the smoke of the incense, with the
prayers of the saints, rose before God from the hand of the angel"
(Revelation 8:4).

In the Gospel of Luke, Zechariah is chosen "by lot" from among his
section of priests to offer incense in the sanctuary (Luke 1:9). Chosen
from among many, not merely a few. This is his time to raise his prayers
to the Almighty.

As Zechariah stands at the altar of incense, an angel appears to him and announces that his wife, Elizabeth, is going to give birth to a son to be named John. Zechariah finds this difficult to believe. He and Elizabeth are both old, and for all these years she has been unable to conceive.

As the story goes, Elizabeth gives birth to John the Baptist. Zechariah and Elizabeth have been blessed, perhaps because of this offering of incense and their consistency in prayer. "Do not be afraid, Zechariah, for your prayer has been heard" (Luke 1:13).

In the Gospel of Matthew, frankincense is among the gifts that the Wise Men bring, along with gold and myrrh, to honor the newborn King (see Matthew 2:11). This pure, rich offering symbolizes the great value of the sacrifice the Savior will offer for the salvation of the world.

By the eleventh and twelfth centuries, incense was used at the Gospel and the Offertory of the Mass. Today, the *General Instruction of the Roman Missal* states:

> The bread and wine are placed on the altar by the priest to the accompaniment of the prescribed formulas. The priest may incense the gifts placed upon the altar and then incense the cross and the altar itself, so as to signify the Church's offering and prayer rising like incense in the sight of God. Next, the priest, because of his sacred ministry, and the people, by reason of their baptismal dignity, may be incensed by the deacon or another minister.[9]

The priest may also incense relics, an image of our Lord, images of saints used for public veneration, the body of the deceased during a funeral Mass, and the Paschal candle. The five nails in the Paschal candle, representing the five wounds of Christ, are actually incense nails.

Incense has been used during Benediction and exposition of the Blessed Sacrament since the fourteenth century. The heavy smell and the thick clouds of smoke surround our prayers. These prayers are the gifts of our lives, and we present them to God.

::: **WITNESS** *(by Deacon Joe)* :::

Sacramentals can be thought of as outward signs of spiritual occurrences. Incense is one example of a sacramental. Incense stirs the senses of both sight and smell. In the context of liturgical celebrations, it creates a prayerful ambiance.

I had the privilege of assisting the bishop at the Liturgy of the Eucharist that was a part of my ordination to the permanent diaconate. I had the distinct honor of incensing the altar, the gifts, and the various participants in the service. As incense is an expression of reverence and prayer, the opportunity to bless the above with incense was a most humbling experience for me. I was the messenger privileged to demonstrate homage to both the holy objects and people.

The use of incense has scriptural significance. It is mentioned over 150 times in Scripture. The vision of the rising smoke reminds us that our prayers are directed upward to heaven. Revelation 8:4 says, for example, "And the smoke of the incense, with the prayers of the saints, rose before God from the hand of the angel." The sweet aroma of the burning incense reminds us of the sweetness of the place to which we are journeying—our heavenly abode.

Performing the incensation during the ordination liturgy was one of the most profound yet humbling experiences I have ever had. That blessing helped me more fully experience the sacrament as a piece of heaven on earth. On that day when I received the special gifts to proclaim the Gospel, preach homilies, and more integrally serve as a minister in the delivery of the sacraments of the Church, there was a lot to be overwhelmed with and to make me feel the grace of God. Being the minister of the incensation deepened my sense of gratitude to God for all that he has done.

::: GRACE :::

I had witnessed this before, but never had I joined so closely in the celebration. Twenty-nine men were being ordained to the diaconate. Many of these men and their wives had been in our bookstore several times during their three years of preparation, supporting our business with purchases of their books for their classes and of items they needed for their ministry. Many I knew from previous encounters. This celebration was personal.

I ventured in at the last minute and sat directly behind a family I had known since my youth. As it turned out, their daughter had become good friends with my daughter in grade school. I love to see life come full circle.

The rituals of the ceremony were overwhelming, including the vesting and the blessing by the bishop and then the incensing. Chosen from the lot was my friend whose family sat in front of me. He was chosen, much like Zechariah, to incense the altar, to raise the prayers of the faithful.

The smoke rose from the altar and then lingered in the air for the entire service. It was as if there were a cloud over the congregation. All were holy. The thick clouds of smoke surrounded our prayers as they were carried up to heaven. So immersed was I in that cloud that I did not notice the two and a half hours that passed. I was within the prayer being lifted up, blessed with a gift in return for my simple presence.

::: PRAYER :::

Lord, we are among the lot you have chosen. We are called to be your witnesses. We pray that your will may be done. As this prayer makes its way to you, we are in turn grateful for your many blessings.

In reverence, may we praise you and honor you with the gifts of our lives. May our prayers be as an offering of incense, ever lingering in blessing to one another as they rise up to you.

::: **CHALLENGE** :::

The next time you attend a Mass with incense, allow the sight and the smell into your prayer. With the incense, let your prayers rise to our heavenly Father.

Be consistent in prayer.

::: CHAPTER EIGHT :::

Fasting

> If you can stand fasting, you will do well to fast on certain days
> in addition to those prescribed by the Church. Besides the
> usual effects of fasting, namely, elevating our spirits, keeping
> the body in subjection, practicing virtue, and gaining a greater
> reward in heaven, it is valuable for restraining gluttony and
> keeping our sensual appetites and body subject to the law of
> the spirit. Although we might not fast very much, yet the
> enemy has greater fear of us when he sees that we can fast.[10]
>
> —ST. FRANCIS DE SALES

In the second chapter of the book of Genesis, already God calls for a
fast. He tells Adam and Eve that they may eat of the fruit of any tree in
the garden except the tree of the knowledge of good and evil (Genesis
2:16–17). God begins with the first man and woman to emphasize the
importance of self-control. He asks that we control our greed.

Similarly, Catholics fast before receiving Communion. Beginning
with the Council of Carthage in 254 and confirmed at the Council of
Antioch in 268, Catholics fasted from any types of food or liquid from
midnight until the time they received Communion. In 1953, Pope
Pius XII changed the rule to require fasting three hours from food and
alcohol and one hour from other liquids. Pope Paul VI changed that
rule in 1964, to fasting for one hour before receiving Communion from
all food and liquids except for water and medicine.

The law of a fast during the Lenten season began in the early Church
and included all Catholics from age eighteen to fifty-nine. Today, the
requirement is to eat only one full meal and two smaller meals with

nothing between meals. The fast is required only on Ash Wednesday and Good Friday, as opposed to the entire forty days of Lent.

The obligations to fast before Communion and during the Lenten season are meant to be ways of emptying ourselves to better prepare for time with our Lord. We can fast throughout the year to enrich our spiritual lives. Going without allows time and attention for better things. Fasting from the luxuries of this life—such as food, television, and social media—gives us time to work for those in need or pray for those who are sick or dying. It can allow us the chance to listen to God so that we might better know his will.

Isaiah teaches us to use our "going without" for something positive.

> Is such the fast that I choose,
>   a day to humble oneself?
>
> ...
>
> If you remove the yoke from among you,
>   the pointing of the finger, the speaking of evil,
> if you offer your food to the hungry
>   and satisfy the needs of the afflicted,
> then your light shall rise in the darkness
>   and your gloom be like the noonday. (Isaiah 58:5, 9–10)

In Matthew 4, we read that Jesus fasted for forty days and forty nights in the desert. Afterward, he was hungry, "famished," the *New Revised Standard Version* says, and he should have been! In his weakened state, he was tempted. He overcame each of those temptations, showing us how to overcome our temptations today. In return, he was waited upon by angels (see Matthew 4:1–11).

When we fast with the right intentions, for a good cause, we too will receive our reward. May we do all for the greater good.

::: **WITNESS** :::

I believe there is an art to fasting. First and foremost, we have to be in the right frame of mind, and it is helpful to have a purpose or a cause. When Jesus fasted, it was not just because he needed a break from the world.

Some Scripture commentaries point to a relationship between the temptations of Jesus and that of Adam and Eve. Our first parents succumbed to temptation and were then cast out into the wilderness, whereas Jesus chose to go into the wilderness, where he overcame temptation and showed himself as the one to win back our chance at paradise. Jesus prayed that he would do the will of his Father. He emptied himself to take on the trial that awaited him. He overcomes this world in preparation for the next, for the kingdom.

I have had only slight brushes with fasting. Each year after my freshman year of college, I gave up something. And I truly kept my promise. One year, I gave up beer, the next year, cigarettes, then meat, then chocolate. Unfortunately, I did this for no spiritual purpose. I gave up something simply to prove that I could do it, so the opportunity for spiritual benefit was wasted.

Oh, there were temptations—lots of dreams of eating Oreos and Krystal hamburgers, of all things. I proved that I could discipline myself for one year, and in the case of smoking, for the rest of my life.

My challenge was of interest to some of my friends. A couple of years in a row, I got a call close to midnight on New Year's Eve from a friend whose family wanted to know what I was giving up that year. Years of fasting and self-control won me a story and a little attention, but I certainly missed the opportunity of achieving any spiritual good.

::: **GRACE** :::

The rules of fasting during the season of Lent and before the reception of the Eucharist are set for us in canon law. They are obligations. But

Jesus teaches us, through Scripture and the teachings of the saints, that fasting is much more than controlling our intake of food and drink. The art of fasting as a sacramental is to deny oneself for the sake of another. The grace received in fasting is to understand that it is just not about us. All of the temptations that we overcome, all of the prayer, and all of the effort should humble us so that others might benefit.

Every day gives us chances to offer up ourselves for another: giving up that cup of coffee so as to give money to someone in need, forgoing the purchase of a new blouse and participating in the drive at church for school supplies for underprivileged children, offering up a snack and consciously substituting a prayer for a friend. In return, we may receive a smile and sometimes the feeling that angels are watching over us and our loved ones. Always a grace.

::: **PRAYER** :::

Lord, you are the perfect example of fasting for the greater good. Teach us your ways, that we may overcome temptation. Help us to offer up our petty desires and fill them with the needs of others.

Lord, there is so much hurt in the world. Lead us to the solutions. Use us for change. Give us the strength we need to make a difference.

::: **CHALLENGE** :::

Fast at some time other than Lent, and offer your hunger up for someone who is going through a difficult time.

Refrain from buying a new article of clothing or accessory, and give the money to the poor.

Donate clothes and household items to Catholic Charities or some other worthy cause.

CHAPTER NINE

The Stations of the Cross

The pious exercise of the Way of the Cross represents the sorrowful journey that Jesus Christ made with the cross on His shoulders, to die on Calvary for the love of us. We should, therefore, practice this devotion with the greatest possible fervor, placing ourselves in spirit beside our Savior as He walked this Sorrowful Way, uniting our tears with His, and offering to Him both our compassion and our gratitude.[11]

—St. Alphonsus Liguori

The Stations of the Cross are a series of pictures or other images representing scenes of Jesus's passion, beginning with Pilate condemning Jesus to death and ending with Jesus being laid in the tomb—or more recently, with the Resurrection. When we meditate on these scenes, moving physically from one image to the next, we are walking the path with Jesus, the Way of the Cross, the *Via Dolorosa*, the Sorrowful Way. This pilgrimage of prayer is one of the most popular devotions of the Church.

In the fourth century, after allowing Christians freedom to worship in the Holy Land, Constantine commissioned workers to build the Church of the Holy Sepulcher at the site that he believed to be Jesus's tomb. Pilgrimages soon began from the church to the place of Pilate's judgment, with stops along the way believed to be associated with Jesus's journey to the cross. In the fifth century, St. Petronius, the bishop of Bologna, reproduced some of those shrines in a group of chapels built at the Monastery of San Stefano.

In 1342 the Franciscans were appointed guardians of the shrines in the Holy Land, and pilgrimages increased, with the faithful receiving indulgences for praying at the different areas. William Wey visited the shrines from England in 1462. He is credited with the term "stations" as well as with changing the direction of the path—now from Pilate's house to the tomb of Jesus.

In the sixteenth century, Muslim suppression of devotion in the Holy Land prompted Franciscans to build replicas of the stations in Europe. The number of stations ranged from seven to thirty-seven. Devotional books on the Stations of the Cross began to appear. In the seventeenth century, Pope Innocent XI granted the right to put stations inside churches affiliated with the Franciscan order. In 1731 Pope Clement XII allowed stations to be put inside all churches, and he settled on the final fourteen stations. Ten years later, Pope Benedict XIV was urging priests to put the images in their churches, along with the fourteen crosses.

The Traditional Fourteen Stations of the Cross
Jesus is condemned to death.
Jesus carries his cross.
Jesus falls the first time.
Jesus meets his mother.
Simon of Cyrene helps Jesus carry the cross.
Veronica wipes the face of Jesus.
Jesus falls the second time.
Jesus meets the women of Jerusalem.
Jesus falls the third time.
Jesus is stripped of his garments.
Jesus is nailed to the cross.
Jesus dies on the cross.

Jesus is taken down from the cross.

Jesus is laid in the tomb.

Several devotional books now include a fifteenth station recognizing the resurrection.

In praying the Way of the Cross, we recall anew the sufferings that the divine Redeemer endured while going from the praetorium of Pilate to the mount of Calvary and his death for our salvation. A plenary indulgence is granted to the faithful who make the pious exercise of the Way of the Cross.

The gaining of the plenary indulgence is regulated by the following norms:

The pious exercise must be made before stations of the Way of the Cross legitimately erected.

For the erection of the Way of the Cross, fourteen crosses are required, to which it is customary to add fourteen pictures or images, which represent the stations of Jerusalem.

According to the more common practice, the pious exercise consists of fourteen pious readings, to which some vocal prayers are added. However, nothing more is required than a pious meditation on the Passion and Death of the Lord, which need not be a particular consideration of the individual mysteries of the stations.

A movement from one station to the next is required. But if the pious exercise is made publicly and if it is not possible for all taking part to go in an orderly way from station to station, it suffices if at least the one conducting the exercise goes from station to station, the others remaining in their place.

Those who are impeded can gain the same indulgence, if they spend at least one half hour in pious reading and meditation on the Passion and Death of our Lord Jesus Christ.[12]

There are many different vantage points from which we can pray the Way of the Cross. We can choose meditations with which we can best relate, the ones that mimic parts of our lives or help us through difficult crosses of our own. Devotions from Mary's point of view highlight the suffering of a mother watching her son being persecuted and put to death to save others.

St. Alphonsus Liguori, St. Pope John Paul II, and Pope Francis have written devotions that give us insight into the overwhelming love of the Father for his children. We can also find versions in which we walk with Jesus on the road to Calvary and others in which we encounter those whom Jesus met along the way as we would encounter them today. Whatever the point of view, the Stations of the Cross are a powerful meditation of the real life journey of the man who died for the salvation of all mankind.

::: WITNESS :::

Walking the Stations of the Cross at the Shrine of Christ's Passion in St. John, Indiana, was a way for my husband and I to experience the journey to the cross in an authentic setting. We felt as if we had stepped back in time, traveled outside the country, and walked beside Jesus. We witnessed Pilate wash his hands of the conviction of Jesus and heard the cries of the crowd, "Crucify him! Crucify him!" The soldiers nailed together a cross too large for any man to drag up the hill we saw before us. We witnessed Jesus's fall under the weight of the wood, and we saw a tender moment with his mother. How did she endure this agony?

Simeon helped carry the cross, but Jesus fell again and again. And during his struggle, he consoled the women of Jerusalem.

As we walked the path, the summer heat encouraged us to rest along the way. The soldiers would not let Jesus take a break. They pushed him forward until he arrived at his place of crucifixion.

The banging of hammer on nails echoed through the area. We stood next to him on the cross, with the two criminals on either side. We joined with Dismas in begging, "Jesus, remember me when you come into your kingdom."

There was no response for us. Our journey is not over. We must walk this path again and again, and we must continue to ask forgiveness.

We visited the tomb of Jesus and saw that it was empty, so we proceeded to the last station, the Resurrection. Words could not describe how we felt witnessing all that Jesus had done for us to get to this final moment. And even that was not all.

He sends his Spirit. Every day he walks with us and gives us all we need for this journey back to him. Each day we must choose to read his Word, to listen to him, to walk with him. "Were not our hearts burning within us while he was talking to us on the road, while he was opening the scriptures to us?" (Luke 24:32).

::: GRACE :::

Jesus has truly blessed us through those who have preserved the past, so that we can understand and participate more fully in his love for us. He has a way of making all that we read in Scripture and learn from tradition mean something to us today. He gives us the grace to witness people right in front of us who carry their own crosses every day. And he fills our hearts with love, so that we do not stand in the crowd watching but go forward to help others, to give of ourselves, to make a difference.

There are those who have intolerable relationships, who need someone to listen. Those who have children or parents who struggle physically or mentally may need a hand now and then. Think about other people around us: a man with a young family who has only three weeks to live, a mother lifting her daughter from her wheelchair to her car seat multiple times a day, a soldier returning to war, a stranger moving into the neighborhood, a homeless man searching for a meal or a bed.

Most of these people we meet do not feel burdened. They are not cranky or mean or unhappy. Quite to the contrary, many of them feel blessed. They are beautiful examples of the modern-day Way of the Cross. It is truly God's gift of grace to be in their presence.

Sometimes all it takes is a moment, a word, a smile, to help these people carry their crosses. Jesus gives us the grace and his own example.

::: **PRAYER** :::

Lord, we humbly pray your Stations of the Cross. The sweat pouring down your face, the yells from the crowd, the falls, and the nails are all images of your love. Thank you, Lord, for this great love, which we can never merit but which you freely give. "Greater love has no man than this, that a man lay down his life for his friends" (John 15:13, RSV).

As we meditate on your Passion, fill us with the grace to respond to the modern-day crosses of those we see around us. Give us the strength and the courage to step out of the crowd and truly love others. Help us to lay down our time, our money, our preferences, for those in need.

::: **CHALLENGE** :::

Go to a church, chapel, or shrine, and pray the Stations of the Cross, meditating at each one for the intention of someone you know.

CHAPTER TEN

The Cross

I am going to talk to you now about the public crosses, and
I am going to give you the reason for their number, for the
blessings which flow from them, and for the great honor
which the Church pays them. If our interior crosses are so
numerous and if the public crosses, these images of that Cross
on which our God died, are also so numerous, it is that we
may have always present in our thoughts the reminder that we
are the children of a crucified God. We need not be surprised,
my dear brethren, at the honor which the Church pays to this
holy wood, which obtains for us so many graces and so many
benefits.[13]

—St. John Vianney

The cross is a symbol of Christianity. Whether we wear crosses around
our necks or carry crosses in our pockets or hang them on the wall,
when we rely on and give honor to the cross, we testify to our faith. We
are blessed to be Christ's witnesses.

As mentioned in chapter one, on the Sign of the Cross, second-
century Church fathers spoke of the symbol of the cross. Tertullian
referred to Christians as "devotees of the cross" and spoke of the importance of marking the cross on the forehead and the chest to keep away
evil.[14]

St. Helena, mother of the first Christian emperor, Constantine, is
believed to have found the True Cross, the one that actually held our
Lord. Helena converted to Christianity in 312 and turned to living a
simple life. She served the poor and imprisoned and devoted much of

her time to building basilicas and shrines. She made many pilgrimages to the Holy Land and, in 326, organized a dig in the area believed to be where Jesus was crucified.

Helena found three crosses. One of these was declared the True Cross when a woman was healed after touching it. Constantine built the Basilica of the Holy Sepulcher over this area and the area where the tomb of Jesus was discovered. The church was consecrated on September 14, which is celebrated now as the Feast of the Exaltation of the Cross.

There are many different types of crosses. The Latin Cross is the one with which we are most familiar. St. Andrew's Cross is in the form of an X, indicating the type of cross on which he is said to have died. St. Anthony's Cross (the Tau Cross) has the crossbar at the top. The ends of the Passion Cross are pointed, like nails. Then there are the Anchor Cross and the Budded Cross.

The Jerusalem Cross has a large cross in the middle, symbolizing Christ, and four small crosses in each corner, symbolizing the spread of Jesus's teachings to the four corners of the world. Or the five crosses together can symbolize the five wounds of Christ.

Regardless of the shape or size, the cross is a symbol of Christ's crucifixion, his death, his sacrificial love for us. The empty cross reminds us of his victory over death. Thomas à Kempis teaches us, "In the cross is salvation; in the cross is life; in the cross is protection from thy enemies."[15]

::: **WITNESS** :::

We have a program in our diocese, for junior and senior high school students, called Search. The program is a weekend retreat that consists of talks by peers and parents, group sharing, prayer, and quiet.

After I made my Search weekend in 1977, the priest who organized the retreats, Fr. Arnold, gave me the opportunity to come back and work on subsequent retreats—first on kitchen crew and then as a leader. I simply said, "I do not think I can." He said, "I do." That was enough for me.

Fr. Arnold helped me lead a group, every step of the way. He gave me a seasoned partner and helped me prepare my talk, from beginning to end. This priest squeezed out of me some of the gifts I had bottled up inside. He helped me speak about my beliefs, which normally came out only in the form of jokes, because I was afraid to share my faith. I worried about how others would react, whether friends would accept me.

Fr. Arnold and I remained friends the rest of his life. Whenever we saw one another, he made the effort to check on me and my spiritual life. He always had some kind of positive feedback. I cannot imagine the hundreds of other young people for whom he made a difference.

When I received my Search cross, a Jerusalem Cross, at the end of my weekend, I had no idea what wearing a cross could mean to my life. First, it identified me with hundreds of other young Christians who had made the retreat. Even today, when I see the cross on others, I know we share a common bond, a common mission in Christ.

Second, the cross identified me as a Christian, as one who believes in and follows Jesus Christ, outside of my church and my school. I believe in the cross with all its meaning: Christ is the center of my life, and I am to take him out to the four corners of the world.

::: GRACE :::

On Good Friday, the faithful come to church to venerate the cross. The young altar servers take turns holding the massive wood, one on each side of the crossbar. The people process forward and kiss the means of our salvation.

Our encounters with the cross throughout our lives give us strength as Christians. Through prayer, the cross brings grace—grace to persevere, to love one another, and to overcome daily obstacles.

When we think about our lives in the Catholic faith, many of us probably can remember crosses we have encountered. When we celebrated our sacraments of initiation, we may have received crosses bearing the symbols of the baptismal shell or the chalice or the dove. Some of us received the marriage cross, with the two rings signifying our union—not just with our spouse but with Christ. These crosses strengthen our daily walk.

There are crosses that have impacted my life, such as the Jerusalem Cross from my Search weekend. A large cross stands on the hill in Medjugorje where many believe that the Blessed Mother appeared to six young people in 1981. There I witnessed faithful pilgrims on their knees, old women in slick black Sunday shoes, families, young and old, climbing to the cross.

The crosses we receive, as well as the ones we witness in our lives, give us the grace to carry our own crosses, big or small. Let us receive the grace to believe in the cross and grace to walk with the man who conquered it for our salvation.

::: **PRAYER** :::

Lord, we all search for you. We pray for all who have not yet found you. We pray that we can witness to the truth and help others to understand all that you have done for us. And we thank you for those who have sacrificed their lives to preach your truth and to offer to us the opportunity for salvation.

::: **CHALLENGE** :::

We all know someone who bears the weight of the cross, someone who carries heavy burdens—physical, mental, or spiritual. Just as St. Helena did, find the cross. Take off one you wear and place it before you, or kneel before one on your wall, and there pray for someone you know who is struggling.

::: CHAPTER ELEVEN :::

The Crucifix

> The cross with the image of Christ crucified is a reminder
> of Christ's paschal mystery. It draws us into the mystery of
> suffering and makes tangible our belief that our suffering
> when united with the passion and death of Christ leads to
> redemption.[16]
>
> —United States Conference of Catholic Bishops

The crucifix is a cross bearing the corpus, the image of Jesus Christ.
In the Catholic Mass, a crucifix is required on or near the altar. Many
churches have large crucifixes hanging on the wall directly behind the
altar.

Although the Council of Constantinople in 629 ordered that Jesus
be shown on the cross in his human form, the crucifix did not become
popular until the Middle Ages. Jesus was usually depicted as the resur-
rected Christ, with his eyes open. In the thirteenth century, the body
was depicted as bloody from the obvious time spent in suffering. Not
until the fifteenth century was Jesus depicted with his head down, his
hands outstretched, and his eyes closed, much like the images we see
today.

The San Damiano Crucifix

Around the twelfth century, St. Francis was a young man at loose ends,
wandering aimlessly throughout Italy and visiting churches randomly.
One day, he passed the little Church of San Damiano, and something
made him enter. The place was dark except for a light that shone on the
painted image of the crucifix. Francis was praying before the crucifix in
the church when he heard the words from Jesus to rebuild the Church.

Today, the original San Damiano crucifix hangs in the Basilica of St. Clare in Assisi, Italy. The large icon cross is a reminder to us that each day we are called, as was St. Francis, to work for the good of Christ's Church, for the good of the community, for peace in the world.

As we gaze upon the San Damiano Crucifix, the figure of Christ acknowledges the crucifixion, showing the wounds in his hands and his feet and his side. But he is the living Christ, with the halo on his head to replace the crown of thorns and with his arms ascending. The crucifix reveals the paschal mystery: Jesus's passion, death, resurrection, and ascension.

The figures under Jesus's arms are the major witnesses of the crucifixion—his mother and St. John on the right, and on the left Mary Magdalene, Mary the wife of Clopas, and the centurion who said, "Truly this man was God's Son" (Mark 15:39). Beneath Mary and John is the soldier who pierced the side of Christ, traditionally called Longinus. Stephaton, the man who offered Christ the vinegar-soaked sponge, is below the centurion.

At the ends of the cross bars are angels, and at the bottom of the cross are possibly the patrons of the area: Saints Damian, Michael Rufus, John the Baptist, Peter, and Paul. The top of the cross depicts Jesus in a royal garment of the Resurrection and the Ascension. He is welcomed by ten angels.

Some people interpret the black area behind Jesus's arms to be the tomb and the area at his feet to symbolize his descent into hell. The dark red and black colors definitely cause the body of Christ to stand out, to radiate and to shine as does the Light of the World.

From this crucifix, Christ spoke to Francis. And as we look upon his body, he speaks to us all:. "Go, repair."

::: **WITNESS** *(by Catherine)* :::

Each year, at our eighth-grade confirmation retreat, Fr. Ed would guide the confirmands to reflect on scriptural themes of moving from darkness to light. The reflection would close with a candle-lighting ceremony at the baptismal font that included a renewal of baptismal promises by the teens. Afterward, they would disperse in silence to find a space in the darkened worship area for private prayer.

One year, Fr. Ed decided to illuminate the processional cross on the altar during the private prayer time. This resulted in a projected image of a larger-than-life cross on the wall behind the altar. After the retreat, Fr. Ed shared that the image inspired him to place a large, permanent crucifix in that spot. The next July, a beautiful, powerful crucifix was installed. Fr. Ed died the following spring.

The crucifix has become for me a symbol of Christ's love for our parish, which was extended to us through Fr. Ed's commitment to this community. It reminds me of the paschal mystery and the reality that in each death, we are promised resurrection.

::: **GRACE** :::

Jesus speaks to me from the cross. Maybe not words that I can hear aloud, as did St. Francis, but if I listen closely, they are words spoken in my heart. Jesus has a plan for me, and whether I hear it or see it plastered across the wall or feel it within, he will tell me what it is.

I am learning to listen. I sit in the quiet of the chapel, with lights dimmed and spotlights casting shadows from the body of Jesus on the cross.

One morning as I sat, I began listing all that I needed Jesus to do. This led to my questioning the way I was praying. Suddenly I blurted out, "God, what am I doing?"

As clearly as if he were sitting next to me, I heard from within, "You are loving me."

The grace I receive from sitting at the feet of Christ crucified is a grace that is indescribable. And it is open to all. There are many faithful men and women who have prayed before the crucifix and received their vocational callings, answers to life's most difficult questions, the overwhelming feeling of mercy and forgiveness, or just simple, unexplainable joy. Like his mother and St. John and St. Francis, let us listen for the Savior's voice from the cross.

::: **PRAYER** :::

Jesus, there has never been a greater sacrifice than yours on the cross. There has never been a greater outpouring of love for another. You are our salvation. You are our hope.

Help us to remember to come to you on the cross that you carried, to listen to you and to honor and love as you love us.

Prayer before a Crucifix

Good and gentle Jesus,
I kneel before you.
I see and I ponder your five wounds.
My eyes behold what David prophesied about you:
"They have pierced my hands and feet;
they have counted all my bones."
Engrave on me this image of yourself.
Fulfill the yearnings of my heart;
give me the faith, hope, and love,
repentance for my sins,
and true conversion of life.
Amen.[17]

::: **CHALLENGE** :::

Hang a crucifix in a prominent place in your home. Let it be a daily reminder of all that Jesus has done for you by dying on the cross and leaving you the Holy Spirit, who guides you through this life. Take time to touch the feet of the one who loves you.

Pray each day before the crucifix. "Pour out your heart before him" (Psalm 62:8, RSV). He will answer. Maybe not the way he answered St. Francis, and maybe not immediately, but he will answer.

::: CHAPTER TWELVE :::

Bells

Make a joyful noise to the Lord, all the lands!

—Psalm 100:1, RSV

Bells, within the context of the Church, are meant to be a reminder for prayer. Whether rung to gather the faithful for Mass, to alert the congregation during the Consecration of the Eucharist, or to cause us to stop during our busy day, church bells have been serving us since the fifth century.

St. Paulinus, bishop of Nola, introduced small hand bells to the early missionaries as a means to call the monks to prayer. Pope Sabinianus approved the use of bells in monasteries in the seventh century, and soon bells became popular in Europe. By the ninth century, the use of bells had spread to small parish churches.

In the eleventh century, the ceremony of the Baptism of the Bells began in France. Before a bell is hung, the bishop washes it with holy water. He then anoints the outside of the bell with the oil of the sick and the inside with chrism. A censer is placed under the bell, and smoke bellows within it. The bishop prays that, as the bell rings, this sacramental will fight evil, protect from storms, and call the faithful to prayer.

By the thirteenth century, outdoor tower bells were rung at the *Sanctus* during Mass. This alerted those outside the church that the Consecration was taking place. Eventually, a small set of hand bells replaced the tower bells for the Sanctus. The altar server rang these during the elevation of the Eucharist at the Consecration.

The ringing of the Sanctus bells has become optional. The *General Instruction of the Roman Missal* states: "A little before the Consecration, if appropriate, a minister rings a small bell as a signal to the faithful. The minister also rings the small bell at each elevation by the Priest, according to local custom."[18]

The Angelus originated in the eleventh century as an evening bell to call the monks to pray three Hail Marys and to meditate on the Incarnation. The devotion expanded, with the bell being rung for the prayers in the evening, in the morning, and finally at midday. It was not long before parish churches followed the monasteries in ringing bells at 6 A.M., 12 P.M., and 6 P.M. The faithful in the area would stop and pray either the Angelus prayer or three Our Fathers.

In 1964, Pope Paul VI prayed the Angelus publicly each week at St. Peter's, followed by a short homily. Subsequent popes have continued this devotion.

The Angelus

V. The Angel of the Lord declared unto Mary.

R. And she conceived of the Holy Spirit.

Hail Mary, full of grace,

The Lord is with thee;

Blessed art thou among women,

And blessed is the fruit of thy womb, Jesus.

Holy Mary, Mother of God,

Pray for us sinners,

Now and at the hour of our death. Amen

V. Behold the handmaid of the Lord.

R. Be it done unto me according to thy word.

Hail Mary...

V. And the Word was made Flesh. (*All genuflect or bow.*)

R. And dwelt among us. (*All stand.*)

Hail Mary...

V. Pray for us, O holy Mother of God,

R. That we may be made worthy of the promises of Christ.

Let us pray:

Pour forth, we beseech thee, O Lord, thy grace into our hearts, that we to whom the incarnation of Christ thy Son was made known by the message of an angel, may by his Passion and cross be brought to the glory of his Resurrection. Through the same Christ, our Lord. Amen.

Today, we can still hear many church bells throughout cities calling parishioners to prayer and to Mass. Several churches still ring the bells at 6 A.M., 12 P.M., and 6 P.M. for the Angelus, and many use the Sanctus bells during Mass.

::: WITNESS :::

My siblings and I were raised in a well-populated area, and the eight of us spent most of our days with one another and with the other children of the neighborhood. Many days and nights saw football and basketball in the backyard, croquet at the neighbors, wading in the creek, catching crawdads, and watching tadpoles turn to frogs. There were no cell phones. We lived close enough to our neighbors that a good yell out the back door by our mother or a sibling could get us inside for dinner.

For some reason, probably from watching too much *Petticoat Junction* on television, our mom decided to change the call for dinner to a firm shake of a cow bell. It was definitely a novelty in the neighborhood. If we heard that bell, we knew it was for us. That bell gathered us together; it called us to the table to share a meal and to share our day. The bell made us stop what we were doing and go home.

Just down the street was our church. As we got ready on Sundays, the familiar church bells called us to gather together with the families of the neighborhood, to come to the table. Once in the church, we heard the bells as our priest lifted the host in Consecration. The bells joined us in prayer and to share a meal.

Our cow bell did not last long. But we have moved back into our old neighborhood, and we still hear those church bells calling us for Mass. They call us to gather to pray and to share our lives.

::: GRACE :::

Recalling the impact the sound of bells had on my youth challenges me to listen for God's call to prayer. I can hear the church bells from my house each morning. They bring a renewed realization that there is something holy, something powerful, soon to happen all over the world. Those bells are not just a call to prayer but an awakening to the Gospel and to the Consecration.

::: PRAYER :::

Lord, as we hear the church bells, may we become more aware of your presence in the world. There are people who receive Communion every morning and carry you out to others. There are those who hear your Word and share it with others. Let the bells be a reminder for us to go and do the same—to pray and to preach and to be your example to the people we encounter.

::: CHALLENGE :::

On whatever technological device you carry, try setting a slight ding or ring to remind you to say the Angelus or simply an Our Father or a Hail Mary—morning, noon, and night. Can you imagine sitting in a crowded restaurant and hearing a hundred phone alarms go off, reminding all to pray?

CHAPTER THIRTEEN

Candles

You are the light of the world. A city built on a hill cannot be hid. No one after lighting a lamp puts it under the bushel basket, but on the lampstand, and it gives light to all in the house. In the same way, let your light shine before others, so that they may see your good works and give glory to your Father in heaven.

—MATTHEW 5:14–16

Lighted candles remind us of Jesus, who tells us in the Gospel of John, "I am the light of the world. Whoever follows me will never walk in darkness but will have the light of life" (John 8:12). Not only do the light and warmth of the flames honor Jesus, but candles also give us the image of our prayers and our petitions being lifted up to him.

In the Old Testament book of Leviticus, God asked for a perpetual light to be burned in the tabernacle, much like our sanctuary light today. This lamp burned with "pure oil of beaten olives." It was "to burn from evening to morning before the Lord regularly," as "a statute forever throughout your generations" (Leviticus 24:2, 3).

Beginning around the second century, Christians lit lamps in a ritual called *Lucernare*, before their evening prayer service. Many believe this to be the origin of the blessing of the Easter fire, the new fire that lights the Paschal Candle, which stays lit during the fifty days of the Easter season as a symbol of the risen Christ. During the Church year, the Paschal Candle is lit during baptisms. From it, a baptismal candle is lit, and the one being baptized is presented with the light of Christ. The Paschal Candle is also lit for funerals.

During the third century, candles carried in funeral processions, primarily as sources of light in the catacombs, were left to burn at the tombs of the dead. Candles were burned in front of relics, statues, and images of the saints in the fourth century. The first time the candles were used in Mass was about the seventh century, and they were not placed upon the altar until four hundred years later.

In the 1600s, the Church made laws surrounding the use of candles. This was a time when high-ranking officials were guarded by "light bearers" when they were out in public. Since Christ is the most important, high-ranking person in the Church, a light, the sanctuary light, is kept burning before Christ in the tabernacle. This actually started in England in the 1200s but became an obligation for all Catholic churches in the seventeenth century.

Many candles burn inside our churches and in our shrines. Large stands often hold a mixture of vigil candles and votive candles. The larger vigil candles are symbols of waiting or vigilance. The word *votive* means "vow," and these smaller candles are often lit when seeking a favor from God or Mary or one of the saints, in exchange for a vow or a promise. As we see these candles burning, we are reminded as a community that there is someone, usually many, who are in need of prayers.

Candlemas Day is February 2. This is the Feast of the Presentation of Christ, the Light of the world, in the temple. Candles are blessed, and parishioners often take some home for use during storms or difficult times.

The major idea behind the use of candles in our liturgies is the reminder that Jesus is our light on our journey to heaven. He will guide and protect us day and night. He is the burning bush that speaks to us, the "pillar of cloud by day" and the "pillar of fire by night" that leads us through the deserts of life (see Exodus 3:4; 13:21–22). The Holy Spirit lights our flame and wants us in turn to be light to others, until the whole world is ablaze.

::: **WITNESS** :::

On every pilgrimage I have ever been on, and even on trips with the family that included visits to a sacred place along the way, there have been opportunities to light candles for our petitions. I am fortunate to have journeyed to Lourdes in France and Fatima in Portugal, two of the most visited pilgrimage sites in the world. There my fellow pilgrims and I lit long tapered candles at the apparition sites. We left them with Mary, along with our requests for our families and friends as well as ourselves.

As I traveled the United States to visit the many beautiful Marian shrines closer to home, I learned about candelariums. These are large rooms filled with candles, which are lit by pilgrims for the intention of or in memory of someone. Our Lady of Guadalupe Shrine in Wisconsin has a chapel with stained-glass windows depicting the apparitions of Our Lady. It is filled with candles lit by those who have visited.

We have lit candles at the Miraculous Medal Shrine in Missouri, Our Lady of the Snows in Illinois, the National Shrine in Washington, and Our Lady of Czestochowa in Pennsylvania. While visiting the Shrine of Our Lady of San Juan de Los Lagos in Texas, my daughter Beth and I decided to go behind the altar with the other pilgrims to pray before the huge image of Our Lady.

Outside the church, we had purchased a candle to light for our special intentions. As we turned a corner on our way to the image, we noticed lines of people waiting their turn for places to kneel. We did the same. Families would light the candles from another candle near them and then spend time in front of Our Lady with their candle. As they finished and moved on, workers gathered their candles and put them on carts, to wheel them to the candelarium. There, the prayers would remain for the six or seven days that the candles lasted.

The faith of the hundreds of thousands of people who visit shrines, both local and abroad, is nothing less than beautiful. Many people tell us that they are following the examples of their parents and grandparents in lighting candles for intentions. Others say that they are lighting candles because they are in desperate need of help.

All agree that there is no magic in the candles. The candles are all about faith in God and prayer. The physical lighting of a candle and leaving it before Jesus or his mother or one of the saints are expressions of that faith.

There is something comforting about seeing the flame in the midst of our times of trial. Jesus is our light in a darkened world. His light, his life on this earth, guides and protects us on our journey.

::: GRACE :::

Many times my family has asked for money to drop as a donation to light a candle. Many times we have witnessed workers within the churches swapping out empty candles and replacing them for new intentions. Millions of candles are lit all over the world, with prayer intentions lifted up by believers.

This is the grace: Every light burning is a prayer. Every flame is about a person who is prayed for, as well as the faithful who struck the match, who ignited the flame, who trusted in the power of prayer. As I think about the grottos where I could barely place my candle because of the intensity of the heat, I realize that the flame is alive.

::: PRAYER :::

Lord, may we be light that burns for your glory. As we light candles and pray for one another, may we help to lead others to you. Light our paths, and guide us on our journey.

You are our light and our salvation. May we follow you, and may our lives be filled with the intensity of your love.

::: CHALLENGE :::

Light a candle at a church or chapel or shrine, and say a prayer for someone in need. Then say a prayer for all the intentions represented in the other flames before you.

CHAPTER FOURTEEN

Holy Oils

Are any among you sick? They should call for the elders of the church and have them pray over them, anointing them with oil in the name of the Lord.

—JAMES 5:14

Scripture refers to oils for everyday use, such as cooking and lighting lamps (see 1 Kings 17:8–16; Matthew 25:1–13), but also shows oils used for strengthening, for healing, for blessing, for consecration, and for sacrifice (see, for example, Exodus 27:20–21; 29:7; Psalm 23:5; 45:7; Mark 6:13).

The early Church adopted the use of chrism for the sacraments of confirmation, baptism, and holy orders. Chrism is also used to consecrate the bells, the baptismal water, the church, and the metal ware for the Mass, as explained by the Church fathers as early as the third century. On Holy Thursday, priests gather in their dioceses as the bishop blesses the chrism and the oils of the catechumens and of the sick. These oils are used by priests, deacons and bishops for the sacraments.

We are anointed with chrism at our baptism and confirmation. In this anointing, we are called to grow in grace. We are set apart, dedicated to the service of God. And with this calling comes his guidance, his gentle touch, his nudge, if we but believe and trust. Often easier said than done.

There are also oils used in praying for the intercession of the saints. Some of these are believed to have exuded from the saints' relics. In the eighth century, St. Walburga helped St. Boniface in missionary work in Germany. When she died, she was buried in Heidenheim, but her remains were later moved to Eichstadt, in Bulgaria. There, oil flows from the stone slab that holds her relics. The Sisters of St. Benedict collect the oil in a silver cup and distribute it in vials to the faithful in need.

In the fifth century began the custom of pouring oil over the relics of saints and collecting it in vials and cloths. This oil was used in praying to the saint for people in need of spiritual and physical healing. The faithful also use oil that is blessed in honor of a saint.

In the nineteenth century, the body of St. Philomena was enshrined in Mugnano del Cardinale, Italy. As was customary, a lamp of oil was left to burn in honor of the saint. A woman from the town came to visit the shrine and, before leaving, dipped her fingers in the oil and anointed the eyes of her blind child. The child's sight was restored. Today pilgrims bring oil to the Sanctuary of St. Philomena, and the bishop blesses it for distribution all over the world. The sanctuary offers very specific instructions that the oil is to be used "within the prayerful intention of the Church as a sign of divine blessing and an expression of faith."[19]

The Church offers careful instruction on the use of oils. A 1997 directive, "On Certain Questions Regarding the Collaboration of the Non-Ordained Faithful in the Sacred Ministry of Priest," formally issued by the Congregation for Clergy and cosigned by several Vatican congregations and councils, states:

> In using sacramentals, the non-ordained faithful should ensure that these are in no way regarded as sacraments whose administration is proper and exclusive to the Bishop and to the priest. Since they are not priests, in no instance may the non-ordained perform anointings either with the Oil of the Sick or any other oil.[20]

::: **WITNESS** *(by John)* :::

The Old Testament speaks to the essential benefits of oils for our physical, emotional, and spiritual well-being. The symbolism— sanctification, strengthening, beautification, dedication, consecration and sacrifice—is rich. But the biblical history of the use of oils is only part of my acquaintance with them. It is an intimate experience with the sacramental ritual that has left a mark on my spiritual journey.

The Church dictates that oils blessed at the Chrism Mass be dispersed to parishes each Holy Thursday. Unused sacramental oils from the prior liturgical year are collected and buried. The cotton cloths used in their administration are burned.

One Saturday in Lent, a friend called and asked if I would help him and some other people bury unused sacramental oils collected from all the parishes in our diocese. I had never been asked to do anything like this before, and I quickly agreed to help.

Our group chose what seemed a most appropriate burial place: a newly erected Stations of the Cross, nestled in the beautiful rolling hills of Camp Marymount, a diocesan Catholic summer camp located just outside of Nashville. We chose the stations at which healing oils may have been used to soothe our Lord: Station 6, Veronica wipes the face of Jesus; Station 9, Jesus falls for the third time; and Station 14, Jesus's body is placed in the tomb.

What began as a simple task became an experience of God's grace. As we poured the oil into the shallow, wide holes that we had dug at the foot of each of the three stations, we prayed the rosary, reflecting on the suffering that Jesus endured for us. Hands outstretched, we prayed for his continued blessings on the oils that brought momentary comfort in his last moments of life. And we prayed especially for people in need of healing, sanctification, comfort, and peace.

Later, we built a bonfire to burn the cloths that had been used in anointings throughout the year. We shared with one another how extraordinarily blessed we were to be picked by our Lord for what we had just done. Friends came out to the camp to share our joy—the joy of being in God's presence, doing his work, and celebrating what it means to be a child of God. It was a spiritual mile marker I'll never forget.

::: GRACE :::

A gentleman comes into our bookstore often and purchases holy cards and pamphlets and Bibles to hand out to anyone interested or anyone in need. He'd tell you we are all in need.

One Saturday, he was quite persistent that I order Philomena oil for him to give to some people in need of a special blessing. I really did not want to deal with it, but I went to the office and placed an order from the shrine in Italy. The oil came in a few weeks later. I got it to the gentleman, and all was well.

In the meantime, a friend from the old neighborhood had a nephew in great need. At nine years of age, he had had what doctors believed was a stroke. Immediately, schedules were coordinated online for round-the-clock prayer before the Blessed Sacrament for this boy. I was simply asked to print prayer cards so that all could pray the same intercessory healing prayer. People in different states were praying together for a life.

The next time the gentleman was in the store, I shared with him the story of this young boy and all the amazing God incidences that had occurred surrounding his family. He said, "You should send them some oil from St. Philomena."

I said, "No, no, it's OK." But he insisted.

I am not like this. Yes, I will pray for this child. I will spend time before the tabernacle. But don't make me send this oil. So I went about my business and forgot about the oil.

When I got home, the update to the young boy's condition was on my computer. I pulled it up and read about him, as well as his family. His sister's name was Philomena! I blinked and stared at the screen. *Philomena.*

The following Saturday, the gentleman came into the store, and I told him what had happened. He reached in his pocket and pulled out his last full bottle of oil. I took it to the young boy's aunt, who planned to see him in the next couple of days.

I am told that many, many stories of God's presence surround this boy and his family. What a witness they are to those they meet! Pure grace.

::: PRAYER :::

Lord, offer us opportunities for grace-filled moments. Help us say yes each day to the anointing of our baptism and confirmation. Guide us with your gentle touch, and lead us in your service, to grow in grace. Teach us to be open to your call.

::: CHALLENGE :::

Read through the rites of baptism and confirmation, especially considering the rite of consecration with the chrism.

CHAPTER FIFTEEN

Holy Water

I will sprinkle clean water upon you, and you shall be clean from all your uncleannesses, and from all your idols I will cleanse you. A new heart I will give you, and a new spirit I will put within you; and I will remove from your body the heart of stone and give you a heart of flesh. I will put my spirit within you, and make you follow my statutes and be careful to observe my ordinances. Then you shall live in the land that I gave to your ancestors; and you shall be my people, and I will be your God.

—Ezekiel 36:25–28

Holy water, water that a priest has prayed over and blessed, is used in the sacrament of baptism as an outward sign of cleansing and purification. Just as water hydrates and nourishes our bodies, so too does holy water nourish our spiritual selves.

Holy water is used throughout our Catholic lives as a means of blessing and of repelling evil. The priest sprinkles the faithful with water at Mass during the Easter season. We sign ourselves with holy water from the fonts as we enter church, a chapel, or even our homes. In this we recall our baptism, renewing our covenant with God and remembering God's forgiveness of our sins and love for us. We also use holy water to bless our homes and other places, to keep them safe from the evils of the world, the flesh, and the devil.

In early Christianity, the water used for baptism was in large bodies, such as the sea or a lake or a flowing river. From the fourth century, there are mentions of using holy water blessed during Mass to sanctify and to heal. In the ninth century, Pope Leo IV ordered that each priest bless water every Sunday and sprinkle the faithful during Mass. Those who wanted to could take home some of the holy water to bless their homes, their fields, their animals, and their food.

During the Middle Ages, the idea that holy water held great powers of healing caused churches to install covers over their receptacles with locks to prevent unauthorized use. The Church has always fought notions of the sacramentals having any kind of magical powers. She has stressed that the sacramentals are purely about receiving grace through the prayers of the Church.

Today, as we put our hand in the holy water or feel the drops from the sprinkler and make the Sign of the Cross, we remember our baptism. We renew our promise to reject sin and affirm our belief in the Trinity, the Church, and life everlasting. Holy water reminds us of the gift of God, the gift of his grace and mercy.

As we enter church and dip our fingers in the holy water font, we leave the outside world and enter into the sacred. "The water that I will give will become in them a spring of water gushing up to eternal life" (John 4:14).

::: **WITNESS** *(by Sarah)* :::

I was so excited for Easter Vigil. The RCIA process had been incredible in itself, but the vigil was the night when I would be starting fresh. I was thirty-one and being baptized, which I had been rather embarrassed to admit until Fr. Steve Wolf informed me that Jesus was around thirty when he was baptized. I thought, "Wow, that's pretty amazing!" It made me connect myself to Jesus's humanness so much more. After that, I was proud to share with anyone who inquired that I was a catechumen.

As I walked to the baptismal font, I saw my family and friends there, and suddenly I became overwhelmed with emotion. Tears just flowed and flowed. One fellow catechumen joked later that I must have had something in my eye. Ha! I was a mess.

We had fourteen in our RCIA group who were to be baptized that night, and I think I was the fourth one in line. I got to watch a few people go before me. So far, so good. When it came my turn, I got in the water, which was a very comfortable temperature. I knelt down and thought to myself, "This is it. Now, hold your breath and take in this moment."

I wasn't expecting anything extraordinary to happen. I had already changed my heart. I had already made a commitment to live my life in a more Christlike way. I had made many friends in the process who supported and prayed for me throughout my journey. Extraordinary things had already happened. But I won't lie. I was hoping something would happen. So I held my breath.

Fr. Johnston filled the pitcher with water. He said, "In the name of the Father," and poured the water on my head. The moment that the holy water touched my head, it was as if all the air had been pulled from my lungs. I was forced to gasp in as much air as I could while water poured down my face.

"What are you doing?" I thought. "Hold your breath!"

"And of the Son," Father continued.

I gasped another unusually large and loud lungful of air.

"And of the Holy Spirit."

Yet another gasp. I'm sure everyone who sat in the pews near the font were thinking, "That poor girl, she's drowning!"

I rose from the water and felt so peaceful and just happy. All of those sins that had accumulated over the years and weighed on my conscience were washed away. Just like that. I was now a child of God, with whom he was well-pleased. I felt as if I were beaming.

After the service, I asked Father, "So, what was that weird gasping thing that I did?" His answer was very simple, "It was the Holy Spirit. I'm just sure of it."

Every time I dip my finger into the font and touch my head, I make an effort to remember how I felt when I came up from the water. And more often than not, tears well up in my eyes. I never want to forget that extraordinary feeling.

::: GRACE :::

Many times I have listened to a homily and received a teaching from the readings that I had never heard before or that hit me just right for something in my life at the time. When our priest shared the story of Sarah's baptism one Sunday, it truly struck a chord in me about my use of holy water. I had become complacent about entering the church, dipping my hand in the font, and crossing myself. Oh, sure, I made the "purifying myself" connection, but it was slightly halfhearted.

Sarah's story woke me up. Who wouldn't want that gasp every time they dipped their hand into the holy water? What a grace God has given me through Sarah!

The water Jesus gives will become in us "a spring of water gushing up to eternal life" (John 4:14). As we dip our hands in the water, the reminder of our purification can cause us too to gasp. This moment is holy. We are blessed.

::: PRAYER :::

Lord, each time we are blessed or bless ourselves with holy water, may we feel that gasp, that "gushing up to eternal life." Help us to learn from one another and to be open to the gifts each has to give.

Purify our love for you. Cleanse us of our sins, and protect us from the evils of this world.

::: **CHALLENGE** :::

Keep a bottle of holy water in your home for blessing, especially in times of need.

CHAPTER SIXTEEN

Statues

You shall make two cherubim of gold; you shall make them
of hammered work, at the two ends of the mercy seat. Make
one cherub at the one end, and one cherub at the other; of one
piece with the mercy seat you shall make the cherubim at its
two ends. The cherubim shall spread out their wings above,
overshadowing the mercy seat with their wings. They shall
face one to another; the faces of the cherubim shall be turned
toward the mercy seat.

—EXODUS 25:18–20

Statues of Jesus, Mary, saints, and angels are meant to remind the
faithful of the lives of those whom God gives us as examples of how
we should live. We do not worship statues. We use statues to recall the
values of a person, to share the lessons of those who have gone before
us, and to help keep our eyes on what's important—the final destination that they have already achieved.

The Old Testament passage above tells us of God's instruction to
build statues of angels atop the ark of the covenant, marking the ark
and its contents as holy. But there are also plenty of warnings in the
Old Testament about statues—specifically against worshipping them.

All worshipers of images are put to shame,
    those who make their boast in worthless idols. (Psalm 97:7)

God knows how easily man is tempted. He knows how words and ideas
can be twisted to serve the desires of man and not him. In ancient
Egypt and ancient Greece, statues were sculpted of pharaohs and

deities, as well as animals, warriors, and famous leaders. The Israelites fell prey to this tendency on occasion. We think of the golden calf they built and worshiped in the desert and their subsequent punishment (see Exodus 32). God's judgment was clear: The Israelites had "acted perversely" (Exodus 32:7).

Once again, we do not worship statues! But these images can draw us toward the sacred.

Not until the medieval and the Romanesque periods, in the tenth and eleventh centuries, did Christian artists begin sculpting free-standing figures to decorate churches. The oldest known statue, from 980, is the golden Madonna of Essen. In the early thirteenth century, rows of statues lined the facades of large churches.

Scenes from the life of Christ—such as the Last Supper and the Resurrection—were sculpted in the fourteenth and fifteenth centuries. In 1499, Michelangelo created his famous *Pieta*. During this Renaissance period, statues increased in popularity as public art and decoration within churches.

Statues of Our Lady grace churches and landscapes all over the world. Some of these are based on descriptions by those who saw her. St. Juan Diego, in 1531 at Guadalupe, Mexico; St. Bernadette, in 1858 at Lourdes, France; and the three children, Lucia, Jacinta, and Francisco, in 1917 at Fatima, Portugal, are some of the most famous visionaries.

The Infant Jesus of Prague Statue

The Infant Jesus of Prague statue is believed to have been made by a friar to whom the infant Jesus appeared. The original statue was made of wax-coated wood, eighteen inches tall. The child holds a globe topped with a cross in his left hand, symbolizing the kinship of Jesus with all the world. His right hand is in the position of blessing, with two fingers up, symbolizing Jesus's humanity and his divinity, and the thumb touching the two fingers, those three digits together symbolizing the Trinity.

Legend tells us that the statue may have been given to St. Teresa of Avila, who gave it to a woman named Dona Isabella. She in turn gave the statue to her daughter, Maria Manriquez de Lara, who took it to Bohemia when she married Vratislav of Pernstyn in 1556. Maria then passed the statue down to her daughter, Princess Polyxena Lobkowitz, who later donated it to the Discalced Carmelites of Prague. She told the friars, "I bring you my dearest possession. Honor the Infant Jesus, and you shall never want."[21]

The friars placed the infant Jesus statue in the oratory of the monastery of Our Lady of Victory Church and prayed before it twice a day. The Emperor Ferdinand II heard about their devotion and sent money each month for the needs of the friary. In 1630, the Carmelites were forced to leave the monastery during the Thirty Years' War. The friary was plundered, and the infant Jesus statue was thrown into a storage area behind the altar.

Five years later, when it was safe to return to Prague, some of the Carmelites moved back into their monastery at Our Lady of Victories Church. It was two years later, 1637, that Fr. Cyril, who had a great devotion to the infant, returned to the monastery. He remembered the statue and found it in a heap of junk stored behind the altar.

The hands of the statue were broken, but Fr. Cyril put it back in the oratory. One day he heard a voice say, "Have pity on me, and I will have pity on you. Give me my hands, and I will give you peace. The more you honor me, the more I will bless you."

Fr. Cyril tried to get the hands of the infant statue fixed several times. Finally, a benefactor paid to have the entire chapel rebuilt, including fixing the hands of the statue. To this day many of the faithful love to pray before the infant Jesus and have experienced the blessings promised.

::: **WITNESS** *(by Sister Mary Angela)* :::

Remembering exactly when and where certain devotions from our childhood began can often bring back sweet memories of our parents' love for their faith. Sr. Mary Angela attests to this:

As I recall, our devotion to the Infant of Prague was actually a parish devotion. My family would go to Our Lady of Perpetual Help Church. The pastor had a devotion to the Infant of Prague, and he taught us to pray to the infant for financial needs.

When I had passed through the stage of playing with dolls, I asked my parents for statues. First I asked for St. Thérèse of Lisieux, then St. Joseph, and finally the Infant of Prague. We had no Catholic bookstore in our area, so a friend of our family whose brother was a priest purchased the statues for us from New Orleans. We had the statues around for years. One appealing part of having the infant statue was that we could change his clothes to match the seasons of the Church.

When I went into the convent, I gave the infant statue away, but a friend bought me a small wooden one. She had seen the statue in our house and knew that it was special to us. When my dad retired and opened an antique shop in Chattanooga, I gave him the wooden statue of the Infant—you know, so his business would prosper. He kept it on a small shelf by his desk, and customers could see it when they came in.

Some years later, when my brother started a company, my dad gave him the statue of the infant. When my older brother died, my dad gave a statue of the infant to the Dominican campus in his memory. He had a great devotion to the infant.

We say the prayers to the Infant of Prague at the convent. Many of the younger sisters had never heard of the Infant, but they learned quickly.

Sr. Mary Angela's sister, Dolly, says the Novena to the Infant of Prague (see "Challenge" at the end of this chapter) and has passed this devotion on to her children. Just as the original statue of the infant Jesus was passed down from generation to generation, so families today pass on the tradition.

::: GRACE :::

As we listen to the many stories of families who have passed down traditions of prayers and faith, we have to consider the importance of that act. Where would we be as a Church if we did not "go into all the world and proclaim the good news" (Mark 16:15)? Jesus gave his disciples the traditions of the Church so that they would preach and teach and spread the Gospel to all generations, and we in turn are to go and do the same.

Families of faith and tradition love to tell stories that remind them of the beauty and richness of the Catholic Church. As we listen to their stories, we too are filled with the grace of their devotion. We can experience the grace of learning about prayer and about witnessing to the faith and about passing that on to our children. Who, if not us, will pass that on? We are responsible, and it is by the grace of God that we remember and that we go and do the same.

::: PRAYER :::

Lord, help us pass along the riches of the faith to our children and to others around us each day. We pray to be good examples. We humbly ask you to use us as you see best, that we may help this generation to turn to you and to see the beauty in the sacramentals as we have received them from others.

::: **CHALLENGE** :::

Pray the Novena to the Infant of Prague for an increase of faith in our world.

Novena to the Infant Jesus of Prague

To be said for nine days or at nine consecutive hours.

O Jesus, who said, "Ask and you shall receive, seek and you shall find, knock and it shall be opened to you," through the intercession of Mary, your most holy mother, I knock, I seek, I ask that my prayer be granted.

(Mention your request.)

O Jesus, who said, "All that you ask of the Father in my name, he will grant you, through the intercession of Mary, your most holy mother, I humbly and urgently ask your Father in your name that my prayer be granted.

(Mention your request.)

O Jesus, who said, "Heaven and earth will pass away, but my word shall not pass," through the intercession of Mary, your most holy mother, I feel confident that my prayer will be granted.

(Mention your request.)[22]

::: CHAPTER SEVENTEEN :::

Medals

I think it is wonderful and wise of the Church to offer sacramentals, faithful holy reminders, to make our faith more tangible—more *real*, if I may say so. Wearing our Miraculous Medal is a holy reminder of a God who loves us immensely and who wants us to live eternally with him in heaven one day. This same God even gave us his Mother as he hung from the cross.[23]

—DONNA-MARIE COOPER O'BOYLE

Religious medals remind us to pray to Jesus and through the intercession of Mary and the saints, the great witnesses of the faith who have gone before us to heaven. Whether we wear a medal as a piece of jewelry; carry a medal in our pockets, purses, or wallets; clip one to our car visors; or hang one around our rearview mirror or on our bedpost, the person that image represents, the example of life and the intercession, helps us in our day-to-day journey. This person stirs in us the desire to live a virtuous life, to take care of our neighbors, and to truly love one another. This is what we treasure in religious medals.

Coins of St. Peter, St. Paul, St. Lawrence, and others are believed to have been in circulation as early as the second century. The newly baptized received medals in the fourth century, and around the fifth century, St. Genevieve was given a medal by St. Germain to remind her of the vow of poverty.

Pope Innocent III, in A.D. 1200, gave permission to priests to have medals cast and distributed to those who made a pilgrimage to St. Peter's. Other pilgrimage sites, such as Santiago de Compostela in Spain and the Holy Land, commemorated visits to their sites with medals as well. Coins called "jettons" were used during this time, as vouchers for attendance at cathedral meetings, identification tags, and other practical purposes. Many of these coins were inscribed with religious sayings or the *IHS* symbol of the name of Christ

In 1566, Pope Pius V began blessing religious medals and greatly influenced the rise of their making and the wearing of them. The blessing practice spread all over the world. By the 1600s, craftsmen in every major city of Europe had begun making medals.

As with all good practices of the faith, the Church continued to stress that the medals and coins are by no means good luck charms. Rather, they are reminders of our duties as Christians.

Today medals are made honoring many of the saints, as well as the apparitions of Mary and the life of Christ. Some of the more popular ones are the St. Benedict medal, the Scapular Medal, the Four-Way Medal, the Miraculous Medal, and the St. Christopher Medal. Many medals are popular because of the saint's patronage: St. Jude and St. Rita for impossible cases, St. Michael for policemen and servicemen, St. Florian for firefighters, St. Gerard for expectant mothers, St. Peregrine for cancer, St. Cecilia for music, St. Nicholas for children, and St. Francis for animals.

The St. Benedict Medal

St. Benedict was the founder of twelve monasteries in Subiaco, Italy. He wrote guidelines for the monks, known as the Rule of St. Benedict. He later founded a monastery at Monte Cassino, Italy, where he died in 543.

In 1880, under the supervision of the monks and at the request of the Very Reverend Boniface Klug, O.S.B., prior of Monte Cassino, the St. Benedict medal was cast to mark fourteen hundred years since the birth of the saint. The medal has the image of St. Benedict on the front, holding a cross in his right hand and the rule for monasteries in his left hand. To his right there is a pedestal with a shattered cup, representing a poisoned vessel that broke when he made the Sign of the Cross over the top. To his left is a raven, about to carry away a poisoned loaf of bread someone had sent St. Benedict.

Above the cup and the raven are the words *Crux S. patris Benedicti,* "the cross of our holy Father Benedict." The Latin words *Eius in obitu nostro praesentia muniamur,* "May we be strengthened by his presence in the hour of our death," trim the outer edge. Directly below Benedict the medal reads, *ex SM Casino MDCCCLXXX,* "from holy Monte Cassino 1880."

The back of the medal has a cross in the center, with the arms of the cross bearing the letters of a Latin prayer, *Crux sacra sit mini lux! Nun quam draco sit mini dux!* "May the holy cross be my light! May the dragon never be my guide!"

In the angels of the cross, we see the letters C.S.P.B., which stand for *Crux S. patris Benedicti.* Above the cross is the word *PAX,* "peace." The letters *VRSVSMV—SMQLIVB* trim the outside of the medal, indicating, *Vade retro Satana! Nunquam suade nuhi van! Sunt mala quae libas. Ipse venena bibas!* "Begone, Satan! Never tempt me with your vanities! What you offer me is evil. Drink the poison yourself!"[24]

The St. Benedict medal is a reminder to follow Christ, to call on his blessing and his protection, and to pray for the strength to overcome the temptations of everyday life. Benedict is the patron saint of a happy death, of monks, of school children, against kidney disease, and against poisoning.

The Four-Way Medal

The Four-Way medal is cross-shaped, containing four medals within the arms of the cross: the scapular, the St. Joseph medal, the St. Christopher medal, and the Miraculous Medal.

The scapular medal has the image of the Sacred Heart of Jesus on one side and an image of Mary on the other. Often the image of Mary is that of Our Lady of Mount Carmel. In 1910, Pope Pius X declared that after being invested in the scapular, a person could wear a medal in place of the small brown cloth. (See chapter twenty-one for more about scapulars.)

St. Joseph is the foster father of Jesus and the chaste spouse of Mary. He is the patron saint of fathers, workers, carpenters, engineers, and the dying.

St. Christopher is the patron saint of travelers. The legend of St. Christopher is that he met a hermit who lived by a river and who taught him about God. One day Christopher carried a young boy across the river. Christopher noticed that the weight of the child was almost too much to handle. The child turned out to be the Christ child. After they had safely crossed, Jesus repaid Christopher by baptizing him.

St. Christopher was martyred for the faith in the third century. His name means "Christ-bearer." He is said to have carried the weight of the world on his shoulders.

The Miraculous Medal was given to St. Catherine Labouré in 1830, when the Blessed Mother appeared to her in the convent chapel at the motherhouse in the Rue du Bac in Paris. Mary asked Catherine to have the medals made. Our Lady said, "All who wear them will receive great graces."

On the front of the medal, Mary stands on a globe, crushing the snake under her feet. This signifies Mary as Queen of Heaven and Earth and her defeat of Satan and all his followers. The rays coming from her hands indicate the graces she gives to those who ask. Around the edge of the medal are the words "O Mary, conceived without sin, pray for us who have recourse to thee." The date of Our Lady's appearance to Catherine, 1830, is at the bottom of the medal.

On the back of the medal is a cross with an *M* woven through it, showing Mary's devotion to her son and his sacrifice for the world. Two hearts below the cross represent the Sacred Heart of Jesus and the Immaculate Heart of Mary. Twelve surrounding stars stand for the twelve apostles and also recall the verse from Revelation 12:1, "A great sign appeared in the heaven, a woman clothed with the sun and the moon under her feet, and on her head a crown of twelve stars" (RSV).

Mary said to St. Catherine Labouré, "Have a medal struck upon this model. All who wear it will receive great graces." The first medals were made in 1832 and distributed throughout France. Immediately, blessings of grace, peace, health, and prosperity began. As word of these blessings spread, so did the devotion. The medal then became known as the Miraculous Medal.

The Four-Way Medal continues to be a popular sacramental for Christians because of the multiple medals all in one. Sometimes the medals are in a different order, and often there is an image of the Holy Spirit in the form of a dove in the center of the front. People may refer to this as a Five-Way Medal.

::: WITNESS :::

Occasionally in our Catholic bookstore and gift shop, we find a story about the medals we see. One person showed us a small, oval, sterling silver Miraculous Medal, slid behind a blue cloisonné medal embedded with red roses, which had been passed down in the family for generations. Sometimes we send a soldier off to the academy or to war with a St. Michael medal, praying that the archangel will guard him from all harm. Or we sell him a St. Christopher medal for protection as he travels.

One snowy morning, my husband Allen and I were the only two to brave the icy roads. A man and a woman and two young boys came into the store wanting to look at medals. They had come over from Vanderbilt Hospital to take a break from watching over the third son in intensive care. He had been in a serious accident. The parents felt helpless.

The parents wanted medals for the protection of the two older boys. They thought that by protecting these two boys, they were at least doing something. We looked at all sorts of medals. There was the Guardian Angel medal, which I think they took because I insisted. And they took a St. Christopher medal, as their dying son's name was Christopher.

Sometimes it's the physical touch of something holy that gives hope and brings peace and calm. When people do not know what to do or say, they may send a medal, a piece of prayer, the life of someone who understands what they are going through, who has been there themselves. The patron of the cause of which they too suffer must know how they feel. Holding on to them will make things better somehow.

The young boys got medals to wear, and the father got one to carry in his pocket. They were things to hang on to in the long hours ahead.

That was it for Allen and me. We never heard about whether the little boy lived, but we know that we were open that snowy day for just one reason.

::: **GRACE** :::

Religious medals carry with them the story of a life. As we learn the stories, we strive to emulate the greatness they portray. We try to take some small piece of what holy men and women have to offer and pay it forward. That's why we choose to wear medals and to have them blessed.

Medals remind us to pray. They remind us of the holy ones who have gone before us and the ones we encounter each day. We call upon the saints for protection and guidance, and in God's great mercy and love, we are blessed in return.

::: **PRAYER** :::

Lord, may the medals we wear be constant reminders of the lives they depict. While wearing them, may we be blessed through the saints' intercession and protected from harm. Help us to continue to spread the messages of Jesus and Mary and the saints and angels.

::: **CHALLENGE** :::

Purchase some inexpensive medals, have them blessed, and keep them in your car or purse or wallet to give away to anyone in need of a blessing or a prayer.

CHAPTER EIGHTEEN

Pictures

Sacred art is true and beautiful when its form corresponds to its particular vocation: evoking and glorifying, in faith and adoration, the transcendent mystery of God—the surpassing invisible beauty of truth and love visible in Christ, who "reflects the glory of God and bears the very stamp of his nature," in whom "the whole fullness of deity dwells bodily." This spiritual beauty of God is reflected in the most holy Virgin Mother of God, the angels, and saints. Genuine sacred art draws man to adoration, to prayer, and to the love of God, Creator and Savior, the Holy One and Sanctifier.

—*CATECHISM OF THE CATHOLIC CHURCH*, 2502,
QUOTING HEBREWS 1:3; COLOSSIANS 2:9

Images in art of the saints, Mary, Jesus, and the angels are used mainly to help the faithful stay focused while praying. They are also means of teaching us about the lives of the holy men and women who have gone before us. The details in these images can speak volumes; the colors and the tones of light and dark often have meaning.

We need good examples in our lives. Pictures remind us of how Jesus and the saints lived the virtues. Framed prints, plaques, posters, icons, and holy cards also give honor to the persons they represent. They remind us to ask for the intercession of holy men and women.

Our Lady of Czestochowa

Believed to have been painted by St. Luke on a tabletop made by Jesus, the image of Our Lady of Czestochowa was brought to Jerusalem, where it was discovered by Constantine's mother. In the ninth century, the image was given to a Greek princess as a wedding gift, and later it was given to the Monastery of Jasna Gora in Poland. During a Hussite invasion, the image was stolen, but the horses pulling the wagon refused to move. The picture was thrown down into the mud and Our Lady's face was slashed by the sword of a soldier. The image has been repaired more than once, but the slash marks always remain on Our Lady's face.

The painting is about four feet high, painted on wood, similar in look to an icon. Mary makes a gesture toward her son, taking the attention off herself. She is dressed in blue, the color associated with humanity. The blue mantel is covered with gold-colored fleur-de-lis, which many view as a lily, the sign of purity. The Child Jesus extends his right hand in blessing, as his left hand holds the book of the Gospels. He is dressed in red, the color of divinity and martyrdom. Both Jesus and his Mother wear gold halos.

Many miracles have been attributed to Our Lady of Czestochowa. She is known as the protector of Poland. St. Pope John Paul II had a great devotion to her.

Our Lady of the Rosary
Blessed Bartolo Longo, a lawyer who returned to the Catholic Church after dabbling in Satanism, traveled to Pompeii to care for the affairs of Countess DeFusco. He found the area to be filled with uneducated, poor, suffering people. As he walked through the local church, he heard a voice that prompted him to promulgate the rosary among the people of the town. He and his wife started a confraternity to Mary and set up rosary festivals.

In search of a picture of Our Lady for devotional use, one of the sisters of the monastery at Porta Medina offered Bartolo an image that had been left in her care by a Dominican priest, who had found it at a junk dealer. The image was of Mary handing rosaries to St. Dominic and St. Catherine of Siena. Bartolo hung the picture in the small chapel, and as people visited and made requests, miracles occurred.

The image was sent to Rome to be repaired in 1965. On its return to Pompeii, it was placed in the Shrine of Our Lady of Pompeii. The shrine has since been enlarged and is known today as the Basilica of Our Lady of the Rosary of Pompeii.

Our Lady of Guadalupe

In 1531, Juan Diego, a Mexican peasant and convert to the Catholic faith, was on his way to Mass when he heard what he thought were birds singing. As he reached the base of Tepeyac Hill, he heard someone call his name and climbed the hill in response to the call. A young woman, surrounded by light, dressed in a blue robe and veil with a pink dress underneath, spoke to him in his native language and asked him to build a church to honor her.

Juan Diego went to the bishop and told him about the woman and her request. The bishop did not believe Juan Diego. Juan Diego reported this to Our Lady, and she told him to try again. The bishop asked for a sign, and Our Lady told Juan Diego to return the next day.

Juan's uncle became very sick, and Juan, on his way to get a priest to give his uncle last rites, tried to avoid Our Lady. But she stopped him and assured him not to worry about his uncle but to climb the hill and pick the roses that he would find. Although it was winter, Juan came down with plenty of roses in his tilma. Mary arranged the roses and sent Juan to the bishop.

Juan was made to wait a long time to see the bishop. Finally he entered the cleric's office, knelt down, and opened his tilma. As the roses fell from the cloak, the image of Our Lady of Guadalupe could be seen on the tilma. The next day Juan Diego showed the bishop where to build the church. The newer Basilica of Our Lady of Guadalupe was completed in 1976.

The tilma shows Our Lady in traditional Aztec dress, with a blue robe covered in gold stars. The pink dress is tied at the waist with the traditional maternity sash. Mary stands on a crescent moon, and a small angel is at the bottom of her robes.

Through the years, the tilma has been examined by scientists, chemists, doctors, and photographers. The fabric has not faded and shows no sign of decay. Mary's eyes reflect the images believed to be the people in the room as St. Juan Diego opened his tilma.

Our Lady gave St. Juan Diego a sign, the image of herself, to remind him and us to come to her in our prayer. She wants us to allow her to intercede for us to our Father. God in turn has left the image of Our Lady of Guadalupe for the Church to venerate.

The Sacred Heart of Jesus

Devotion to the Sacred Heart of Jesus is found in early Church history, mentioned by several of the Church fathers before the fifth century. In the twelfth century, St. Bernard of Clairvaux described the love of Jesus opening to him from the wound pierced in his side during the crucifixion. "Draw me completely into Thy Heart, O my amiable Jesus. Open to me this Heart which has so many attractions for me! What! Does not this pierced side leave an entrance open for me, and does not the open wound of this Sacred Heart invite me to enter there?"[25] Later centuries reveal the devotion in Benedictine, Cistercian, Dominican, and Franciscan monasteries. St. John Eudes made the Sacred Heart of Jesus a public devotion in the seventeenth century.

The honor given to the image of the Sacred Heart as we know it today began after the apparitions to St. Margaret Mary Alacoque in 1673. She explained that Jesus allowed her to rest her head against his chest, as he revealed to her the image of his heart with flames coming from it and a crown of thorns around it, surmounted by a cross. She could clearly see the wound he had received on the cross. He revealed to her that he desired the image to be honored and that those who did as he asked would receive twelve promises:

I will give them all the graces necessary in their state of life.
I will establish peace in their houses.
I will comfort them in all their afflictions.
I will be their strength during life, and above all, during death.
I will bestow large blessings upon all their undertakings.
Sinners shall find in my heart the source and infinite ocean of mercy.
Tepid souls shall grow fervent.
Fervent souls shall quickly mount to high perfection.
I will bless every place where a picture of my Heart shall be set up and honored.
I will give to priests the gift of touching the most hardened hearts.
Those who shall promote this devotion shall have their names written in my Heart, never to be blotted out.
I promise you in the excessive mercy of my Heart that my all-powerful love will grant to all those who receive Holy Communion on the First Fridays in nine consecutive months the grace of final penitence; they shall not die in my disgrace, nor without receiving their sacraments. My divine Heart shall be their safe refuge in this last moment.[26]

Jesus asked St. Margaret Mary to promote this devotion so that all mankind would know his burning love for his children. He requested that homes display his image and people carry small pictures.

Thirty years after St. Margaret Mary's death, a plague spread through Marseilles, killing thousands of people per day. The bishop asked the sisters to make Sacred Heart badges to give to the people of the city.

The faithful processed through Marseilles wearing the badges. In 1789, during the French Revolution, Catholics wore the badges for protection. The Cristeros in Mexico and the Catholic Cubans fighting the government who opposed the Church in the twentieth century, facing execution and imprisonment, wore the badge of the Sacred Heart.

In 1870, Pope Pius IX approved the devotion of the Sacred Heart badge, granting an indulgence to all who wear it and pray daily one Our Father, one Hail Mary, and one Glory Be. The small picture of the Sacred Heart is a reminder of Christ's deep love for us and our responsibility to cooperate in the redemptive work set before us each day, our daily trials. And with this image that we wear—or carry in our wallets or our purses—comes the promise of his blessing. Our names are written in his heart.

In 1899, Pope Leo XIII consecrated the world to the Sacred Heart of Jesus, his physical heart. The feast day is celebrated nineteen days after Pentecost.

At Fatima, Portugal, in 1917, Our Lady appeared to three children, entrusting them to spread devotion to her Immaculate Heart. In 1942, Pope Pius XII dedicated the Church to Mary's Immaculate Heart, and in 1984, St. Pope John Paul II consecrated the world, and specifically Russia, to the Immaculate Heart. The image of Mary's heart is encircled by roses or lilies, with a sword piercing through the middle. Images of the Sacred Heart of Jesus and the Immaculate Heart of Mary are often pictured together.

Prayer by Pope Pius IX

Open Thy Sacred Heart, O Jesus! Show me Its beauty and unite me with It forever. May the throbbing in all the movements of my heart, even during sleep, be a testimony of my love and tell Thee unceasingly: Yes, Lord Jesus, I adore Thee…. Accept my poor little actions…grant me the grace of repairing evil done....so that I may praise Thee in time and bless Thee for all eternity.[27]

::: **WITNESS** *(by Mary)* :::

We were raised with the image of the Sacred Heart in our home. I remember praying the rosary in front of it from the time I was in grade school.

We always knew when our dad had been at the funeral home. When we walked up to the casket, there would be a Sacred Heart badge either in the hand or on the chest of the person who had died. Since the death of my dad, I have started doing the same, but I usually slide the badge into a pocket or down the side of the casket. No one seems to mind. If people question what I'm doing, I show them the badge, and they seem to be fine with it.

My dad would buy those badges by the hundreds. When he caught someone's eye in the grocery store or on the street, he would say, "Here's Jesus. What's your name?" I cannot imagine how many thousands of those he handed out in his lifetime.

One night after he left the grocery store, a couple fellows followed him home to rob him. They approached him right as he got out of his car. He just handed them a Sacred Heart badge and said, "Here's Jesus. What's your name?"

Well, they threw the badge down on the ground, which really upset my dad. They just wanted his wallet. My dad gave it to them but asked them to please leave his license; he was too old to have to go get a new one. Dad firmly believed that the Sacred Heart kept those guys from hurting him in any way.

Dad believed in the mission of the Sacred Heart badge. He wanted others to know Christ—to see his face and to be protected from the evils of the world. He wanted everyone to enjoy the promises of Christ and share in the saving work of redemption.

My dad also loved *The Pieta Prayer Book*.[28] He read it over and over and shared it with everyone. My dad was truly special. He lived a life filled with the love of Christ.

::: GRACE :::

Beautiful images of Jesus and of the Blessed Mother are not difficult to find, but sometimes we need more than just a pretty picture to bring us to our knees, to bring us to prayer. Learning the stories behind the images that represent those people the Church venerates gives us a deeper understanding of the message that Christ and his mother and the saints want us to receive. After all, it's not about the picture but about the person.

What better person to show us his heart than our Savior, who not only died for us but returns to us and remains with us, to give us the opportunity to be with him in heaven. And what better person than his mother to appear to us time and time again and repeat the importance of prayer and fasting and repentance. She teaches us about the repair so desperately needed among the faithful. She reminds us to visit her and to visit her son, and she gives us gifts.

So deep is her love for us that staring at her image can bring me to tears. She truly wants us all. She wants us to love one another and to do the right things, so we can be with her and her son. She is our example, as are the other saints God has sent to help us. Through them we can learn to love and to help one another to love.

::: PRAYER :::

Lord, as we look upon the beautiful images of your son, of Our Lady, and of the saints, help us to see beyond the images and receive the messages you speak through them. Help us to take the time to receive the gifts you promise.

::: **CHALLENGE** :::

Find a picture, a plaque, a holy card, or an icon, and sit with whomever is portrayed. Think about the colors the artist used and the meaning behind the items pictured with the holy one. Take time venerating the person. What is the message?

::: CHAPTER NINETEEN :::

Pilgrimages

Pilgrimage embraces…that strange pause which God seems
to demand of all pilgrims. The pause of total stillness and of
being available to anyone.[29]

—Catherine de Heuck Doherty

A pilgrimage is typically a journey to a holy place, such as a shrine or a
basilica or an area of significance to the faith. Our journey through life
is a pilgrimage. We walk with others, increasing in faith and spiritu-
ality, trying to obtain the final destination.

The Holy Family made the first Christian pilgrimages. They traveled
annually to Jerusalem for the Feast of Passover (see Luke 2:41). Early
Christians made pilgrimages to the Holy Land, to walk in the footsteps
of Jesus, and to the tombs of martyrs, to honor all that those holy ones
had done for the faith. Primary pilgrimage routes of the Middle Ages
included Jerusalem, Rome, and Santiago de Compostela, in the north-
east corner of Spain. Today, the faithful make pilgrimages to places all
over the world where God has worked in miraculous ways.

Lourdes, France

Our Lady appeared to Bernadette Soubirous in 1858 in Lourdes,
France, in the foothills of the Pyrenees Mountains. Pilgrimages are
made every day of the year to the grotto where our Lady appeared.
Faithful volunteers push wheelchairs and strollers from the hospital,
carrying the sick to bathe in the miraculous waters. This water
flows from the same source as did the water with which Our Lady
commanded St. Bernadette to cleanse her face.

Pilgrims walk in an evening procession, fulfilling Our Lady's request
to Bernadette: "Go tell the priests to have people come here in a

procession."[30] They stand on holy ground and pray for the sick and the dying, for family and friends, for our youth and our world. Thousands attend Mass, go to confession, and pray the rosary throughout the day.

Fatima, Portugal

In 1917, Our Lady appeared six times to three children in Fatima: Lucia, Francisco, and Jacinta. As at Lourdes, pilgrims come from all over the world to walk where Mary appeared, to pray the rosary, to attend Mass, and to go to confession. The Apparition Chapel marks the place where Our Lady appeared, with a marble column holding a statue of the Pilgrim Virgin. The faithful say the rosary, crawling on their knees around the apparition site.

Inside the Basilica of Our Lady of the Rosary of Fatima are the tombs of Francisco and Jacinta, as well as stained-glass windows that tell the story of the apparitions. Also inside are fifteen altars, dedicated to the joyful, sorrowful, and glorious decades of Our Lady's rosary. Many of the faithful walk for days in pilgrimage to Fatima, praying the rosary and the Stations of the Cross.

Santarem, Portugal

Not too far from Fatima, pilgrims honor Jesus in the Eucharistic miracle of Santarem. In 1225, a woman unhappy in her marriage went to visit a sorceress, who told her that if she brought her a consecrated Host, her husband would love her again. The woman went to Mass and received the Host, then left the church and removed the Host from her mouth.

On her way to see the sorceress, the woman noticed blood dripping through her hands from the consecrated Host. She ran home and threw the Host into a trunk at the end of her bed. That night, a bright light shone from the trunk, illuminating the entire bedroom. The woman confessed to her husband what she had done, and they knelt together before the Host in adoration until morning.

They called their priest, who took the Host in procession to the church. There it was placed in a wax container and put in the tabernacle. The next day, when the tabernacle was opened, pieces of broken-off wax surrounded the Host, which was now encased in a crystal pyx. The pyx was put into a gold and silver monstrance.

Travelers go to the small church in Santarem today to witness the Eucharistic miracle. The monstrance is displayed for the faithful, high above the tabernacle.

My daughters, my mother, and I entered this dark church several years ago. As we knelt before the tabernacle, a man told us to look above it. There we saw the Eucharistic miracle displayed.

Meanwhile, a woman in a front pew signaled us to go behind the altar. The man brought us back there and allowed us, one at a time, to climb a slim ladder and stand face-to-face with the Body and Blood of Christ. In front of us was a plaque that read, "John Paul II prayed here."

As had many pilgrims before us, we walked in the footsteps of a saint to honor Jesus in his true presence in the Eucharist.

Santiago de Compostela, Spain

The Camino de Santiago, or the Way of St. James, is a pilgrimage route with several possible starting points—mainly in France, Spain, and Portugal. The destination is the Shrine of St. James the Great, apostle and martyr.

Beginning in the eleventh century, and highly promoted in the twelfth century by Pope Callixtus II, the *Camino* follows a Roman trade route to the Atlantic coast of Galicia. Scallop shells found on the shores of Galicia became symbols for the walk. These are seen on posts and signs along the way, and pilgrims also wear them around their necks.

There are five popular routes. The French Route begins on the French side of the Pyrenees Mountains and is 485 miles long. The Silver Route, starting in Seville, Spain, goes north 621 miles. The Northern Route begins in France at Irun and moves along the Northern coastline of Spain, including 513 miles of rough terrain. The Portuguese Route, which is 142.9 miles long, starts in the city of Porto. Finally, the English Road is 47 miles from A Coruna, Spain, or 68 miles from Ferrol, Spain; neither of these two routes is long enough to claim a *compostela*, a certificate of completion.

More than a hundred thousand *compostelas* are given each year to pilgrims from all over the world. The name of each pilgrim who attends Mass in the Cathedral of Santiago de Compostela, celebrated daily at noon, is announced, along with his or her country of origin and pilgrimage starting point.

::: **WITNESS** *(by Jim)* :::

I became Catholic thirty-four years ago. I wasn't raised in a church, so most of my intimate experiences with my Lord have been through the Catholic Church—Marriage Encounter and Cursillo being the most profound.

I am preparing for retirement, so when my friend Fr. Mark Beckman mentioned that he was planning to hike the *Camino de Santiago*, I was intrigued. What better way to prepare for this next stage of life than with my friend and pastor and two other men, hiking five hundred miles on a spiritual pilgrimage?

Although we all trained vigorously for months, I knew that walking fifteen miles a day was over my head—and that was the profundity of the spiritual experience for me! Spending these hours with God, leaning on him for strength and peace, seeing his face and hearing his voice through the countless strangers with whom we shared our journey: This is what my pilgrimage on this earth is meant to be! I learned the beauty of listening to the stories of others before I shared mine. I learned that serving them was more rejuvenating than any rest I could imagine.

I experienced, at my core, peace and joy, even when my bones ached and my feet were blistered. Christ's strength infused me through the joy, laughter, and support of my fellow pilgrims. This next stage of my life will be richer because of this humble walk.

::: GRACE :::

As we reflect on our pilgrimage on this earth, we come to the understanding that it's not all about us. Even when we travel on a physical pilgrimage, we learn that it's not necessarily about the journey. Pilgrimage is about encounter.

God gifts us with one another for our journey, this pilgrimage to heaven. He awakens us to the gift of encounter, allowing encounters, good and bad, to enrich us and push us to do more, to go outside ourselves. That is grace.

::: PRAYER :::

Lord, give us strength for the journey. Whether we are traveling to a beautiful pilgrimage site or down the busy streets of our own hometowns, fill us with the gift of the encounter. May we be humbly blessed to be a gift to someone else in return.

::: CHALLENGE :::

Go on a pilgrimage. It does not have to be an elaborate trip. There are many holy sites right in the United States. (See my book *Visiting Mary: Her U.S. Shrines and Their Graces* if you want some ideas!)

::: CHAPTER TWENTY :::

Relics

We...refuse to worship or adore the relics of the martyrs.... For we may not "serve the creature rather than the Creator, who is blessed for ever." Still we honour the relics of the martyrs, that we may adore Him whose martyrs they are.[31]

—St. Jerome

Relics are ashes, bones, clothing, and objects connected with a saint or holy person, preserved and enshrined to be venerated. Relics are typically classified as first class, actual parts of the saint's body or instruments of his or her torture, in cases of martyrdom; second class, items that have come in close contact with the person, such as clothing and personal items; and third class, things that have touched the body of the saint or the first or second class relic.

Scripture tells of the relics of Elisha bringing a man back to life:.

> So Elisha died, and they buried him. Now bands of Moabites used to invade the land in the spring of the year. As a man was being buried, a marauding band was seen and the man was thrown into the grave of Elisha; and as soon as the man touched the bones of Elisha, he came to life and stood on his feet. (2 Kings 13:20–21)

We read in Acts 19 that God used items that had touched St. Paul to heal: "God did extraordinary miracles by the hands of Paul, so that handkerchiefs or aprons were carried away from his body to the sick, and diseases left them and the evil spirits came out of them" (Acts 19:11–12, RSV).

In the second century, after St. Polycarp was burned at the stake, the faithful gathered his bones in order to have them available for veneration upon the anniversaries of his death. From the fourth century come mentions of miracles occurring from the bones and other relics of the saints. St. Jerome made it known that no power came from the relic itself; the power comes from God alone.

Many believe that when St. Helena uncovered the three crosses on Mount Calvary, she determined which one was the True Cross of Jesus Christ by touching all three to a sick woman. The first two crosses did nothing, but the third cross cured the woman.

The Second Council of Nicaea, in 787, made the decree that every altar should contain a relic. Today, altars in Catholic churches still contain one or more relics of saints.

During the Middle Ages, relics were put into reliquaries and honored. However, as the number of relics increased, so did the abuse of selling relics, both authentic and forged. This led to skepticism by the faithful.

In the sixteenth century, the Council of Trent defended the veneration of relics. From that arose a renewal of preservation of relics for the purpose of veneration. Today, many third-class relics can be found encased with medals and holy cards.

::: **WITNESS** *(by Philip)* :::

Around 1960, a priest on pilgrimage in Rome brought the relic of St. Philip the apostle back from the Office of Relics and gave it to Sr. Mary Philip, O.P., at the St. Cecilia motherhouse. Sr. Mary Philip gave the relic to my aunt, Sr. Philip Joseph, who wore the relic over her heart. One day it ended up in the wash. Before it was retrieved, the reliquary filled with water, and the glue was dissolved.

I received the relic by mail, in a package that had been cut open and examined by the post office, as if it were some type of contraband! I don't know how it got to me—but by the grace of God. When I pulled it out, I thought, *Wow! I can really see this little bone, this bone that was in the boat on the Sea of Galilee, at the feeding of the five thousand, and in the Upper Room at the Last Supper.* This was the St. Philip we read about in the Gospels and in the Acts of the Apostles. This was one of the Twelve.

I may never know the full extent of the graces I received while this relic of St. Philip was with me. Coming to truly believe and understand, to a small extent, the nature of the Eucharist was one of the most humbling. This bone is a part of a man who sat at the table in the Upper Room. And so I do today. I don't know how to explain it exactly, but when I looked at that relic, no time was involved. There was no two-thousand-year separation. I was right there. All doubt, all notions of symbolic nature and ritual habit were eliminated.

Jesus Christ is alive and risen and truly with me continually within the Eucharist. Every time I participate in the Sacrament, I am alive with Christ. It is a renewal of God's promise, the new covenant alive within me. It is holy and humbling. I am privileged to participate in God's call in such a personal and intimate manner.

I will say that having a first-class relic in my possession is not like owning it but more like having a person in my care. For Sr. Philip Joseph, to give that care up was a true testament to her vows. That she could pass something so precious on to someone else speaks well of her humility and faith.

I had had the relic in my care for several years when the elderly Msgr. Rohling needed help with Mass at the nursing home. We would set up a table in the lunch room of West Meade Place for him to use as an altar. Because this *ad hoc* altar did not have an altar stone containing relics of saints, I was able to put the relic of St. Philip on the altar with him as he said Mass.

One day, as I was putting Msgr. Rohling's sandals on his feet, I looked up and saw in his face the line of faces of those ordained before him. It was an ordination line, all the way back to St. Philip the apostle. I realized that St. Philip was with this holy priest in a special manner during this last phase of his life on earth. When Father was too sick to say Mass, I would sit with him, pray the rosary with him, and set the relic on his chest. He would move his hands as if he were saying Mass. Always a priest.

When my cousin Philip lost his brother in a sudden accident, I sent the relic to him. As I said, having a relic is not like owning it; it's more like having someone in your care. I felt that my cousin needed St. Philip more than I did at the time.

When St. Philip the apostle was in my care, I learned deeper lessons in God's love, forgiveness, humility, and selflessness. I knew St. Philip was with me, as a teacher and a mentor. I will be forever grateful for the privilege of his presence in my life, always directing me toward Christ.

::: GRACE :::

More than once, my eyes filled with tears as Philip poured out his heart about the gift of the relic and how it affected his life and the life of one of our priests. He went on to tell about holy water that Monsignor had given him and the blessings it brought at the deaths of two close relatives. He shared the importance of the stained-glass windows in our church. On one side are pictured the seven virtues, and on the opposite side, the seven deadly sins. His pastor had explained the importance of walking in the seven virtues to avoid the seven deadly sins.

As this man spoke, I was sitting between the two sets of windows. I considered how we humans tend to bounce back and forth, from side to side. But behind me in the church was the huge Good Shepherd stained-glass window, and in front was the altar. We have to believe and to trust that God has us. His grace connects us.

We cannot focus on two sides of the church at the same time, so we focus on the virtues. We also allow the Shepherd to keep us focused on Christ in the Eucharist. Sometimes Christ the Good Shepherd works with us directly, sometimes through the pope, our bishops, and our priests.

What a gift it was to spend time with Philip, whom I did not really know that well. His story of relics brought us together, and the gift of Christ keeps us connected. Let us all be open to one another's stories, so we can receive the gifts of grace that God has to give us through one another.

::: PRAYER :::

Lord, you offer us reminders, bits and pieces of the past, of holy men and women. May we reverently use them as blessings for our lives. May we share these blessings freely with others, passing them on so that all may be blessed and all may rejoice in the beauty of the Church.

::: CHALLENGE :::

If you have the opportunity to view a relic, go and sit in its presence. Allow a saint to teach you how to love and serve God.

Let go of something you treasure, something that has blessed and inspired you, and give it to someone. Allow it to bless that person's life.

::: CHAPTER TWENTY-ONE :::

Scapulars

> It is not uncommon for devotion to Christ, Mary and the saints to include material objects, from pictures to scapulars to relics. The material object has often given to the devotion its title.[32]
>
> —*CATHOLIC SOURCE BOOK*

The word *scapular* refers to either the monastic scapular or the devotional scapular. The monastic scapular is a long piece of material worn like an apron by religious orders. It is an outer cloth, the width of the chest, which hangs down the front and the back of the religious, almost to the feet. The Rule of St. Benedict, from the seventh century, refers to the scapular as part of the religious habit.

The devotional scapular is made up of two small pieces of cloth, wood, or laminated paper, upon which are portrayed religious images. The cloths are joined by ribbon, rope, or string, so that the scapular mimics the monastic scapular. One cloth typically hangs down the front to a person's chest, and the other piece hangs down the back.

The most popular devotional scapular is the brown scapular, also known as the Scapular of Our Lady of Mount Carmel. Our Lady appeared to St. Simon Stock in Cambridge, England, in 1251, as he prayed for help for the oppressed Carmelite Order. Our Lady presented him with the scapular and told him to wear it in order to receive special graces. She promised that whoever died wearing it would not "suffer eternal fire."[33]

The Blue Scapular of the Immaculate Conception was revealed to Venerable Ursula Benicasa, who founded the Theatine order of nuns.

When Jesus promised her order special graces, including the conversion of sinners, she asked him to extend those promises to the faithful outside the order who wore the scapular in honor of the Immaculate Conception.

There are many other types of scapulars from the different monastic orders, all worn to honor Jesus, Mary, and the saints. Many have promises and indulgences attached.

The Red Scapular was given to a Sister of Charity of St. Vincent de Paul, with the promise of an increase of faith, hope, and love for those who contemplate the passion of our Lord.

The Scapular of St. Joseph was given to the Capuchin order, to remind wearers of St. Joseph's humility and purity and to ask the saint to intercede for the Church and assist at the hour of death.

The Black Scapular of the Seven Sorrows of Mary is worn by members of the Servite order, dedicated to bringing devotion to Our Lady's sorrow during the passion of her son.

The Scapular of the Blessed Trinity, a white scapular with a blue and red cross, is given to the faithful who want to be associated with the Trinitarian order, devoted to the Holy Trinity.

The Five-Fold Scapular includes the Red Scapular, the Scapular of the Blessed Trinity, the Brown Scapular of Our Lady of Mount Carmel, the Black Scapular of the Seven Sorrows of Mary, and the Blue Scapular of the Immaculate Conception.

Devotional scapulars grew in popularity around the seventeenth century. To wear the scapular and share in the promises and the indulgences it carries, a person must have it blessed and wear it continually with proper, faithful intention. Some scapulars require that a person be vested in them.

The Green Scapular

The Green Scapular is made of only one piece of cloth attached to strings. In 1840, Sr. Justine Bisqueyburu, a Daughter of Charity of St. Vincent de Paul in France, received private visions of the Blessed Mother as she prayed. Mary was dressed in a white gown with a blue mantle but no veil. She held a burning heart in her hand. Sr. Justine believed that the visions were intended to increase her personal devotion to the Immaculate Heart.

But the next time Our Lady appeared, she held what looked like a scapular in the hand opposite from her heart. On one side of the cloth was Our Lady's picture as she appeared to Sr. Justine; on the opposite side was her pierced, flaming heart with the words, "Immaculate Heart of Mary, pray for us now and at the hour of our death." An interior voice explained to Sr. Justine that Mary wanted her to distribute these scapulars for good health and the conversion of souls. Those who wore them or had them on their person would also obtain a peaceful death.

After many attempts to have the scapulars made and to spread the devotion, Pope Pius IX finally granted permission for their use in 1870.

::: **WITNESS** *(by Sister Clare Therese)* :::

In 1957, a few months before entering the Dominicans, I was a sophomore at the College of Mount St. Vincent and living in the Bronx with my parents. Although both my parents were baptized Catholics, they had long since abandoned the faith. One of the Sisters of Charity at the Mount gave me a Green Scapular to give to each of them.

During my novitiate, my parents divorced, and my father returned to his family home in the Catskill Mountains. There, in late 1959, he died suddenly at work. At the wake, my aunt told me that recently Dad had agreed to talk to a priest. God must have been satisfied with this intention, since he called my dad before he could see the priest.

My aunt went on to say that I might want to keep something that was found in my dad's pocket. She handed me the Green Scapular, with its precious inscription: "Immaculate Heart of Mary pray for us now and at the hour of our death." Needless to say, this sacramental is now in my pocket, and I am confident that Our Lady will take care of me as I believe she took care of my father.

::: GRACE :::

Jesus has a way of allowing others to work in us when we least expect it. Speaking to others about sacramentals has reawakened many stories that had been forgotten—not necessarily by the person with whom I was speaking but by others who had no idea when or where or how the gifts of faith in their families started.

The Green Scapular is one of those sacramentals that seem to creep into my conversations with people about completely different things. One woman told me she keeps one under her husband's side of the bed at all times, hoping and praying that someday he will turn his life to Christ. A mom puts Green Scapulars under all her children's beds, even though they are all very much into the Catholic faith right now. "I just want my children to get to heaven." As I shared a few stories with my father, he said, "Oh, yes. I put the Green Scapular in the box my father kept on his dresser, and he finally converted from Baptist to Catholic."

A Dominican sister shared that her mother said aspirations about 150 times a day in remembrance of all the Green Scapulars that had been put in the hands of those who didn't even know what they had. I got chills thinking of this little woman cleaning her house and repeating, "Immaculate Heart of Mary, pray for us now and at the hour of death," over and over for those she knew and those she did not know.

We can all do this: Wear the Green Scapular for the conversion of sinners, for the conversion of the world. Share it with others. And pray this simple prayer to Our Lady. What a difference a minute can make!

::: **PRAYER** :::

Immaculate Heart of Mary, Sacred Heart of Jesus, pray for us now and at the hour of death. Amen.

::: **CHALLENGE** :::

Obtain a scapular. Wear it prayerfully, or carry it on your person.

::: CHAPTER TWENTY-TWO :::

The Rosary

To recite the rosary is nothing other than to *contemplate with Mary the face of Christ.*[34]
—POPE JOHN PAUL II, *ROSARIUM VIRGINIS MARIAE*

The rosary, the actual set of beads, is a physical reminder to honor Mary and her son in prayer. Praying the rosary gives honor to the requests made by Our Lady when she appeared to the children in Lourdes and Fatima.

Many believe that the rosary was developed by early Christians who wanted to pray the 150 psalms daily. Those who were unable to memorize or to read the psalms recited 150 Our Fathers, keeping count on what they called *Pater noster* beads. The prayers later became Hail Marys, and the prayers together were referred to as Our Lady's Psalter.

Around 1208, Dominic de Guzman, a Spanish preacher, traveled to France in order to defend the faith and convert the Albigensians. As he was praying in a chapel at Prouille, Our Lady appeared to him and taught him the complete rosary. She asked that her rosary be preached and popularized. Mary gave Dominic fifteen promises for those who would pray her rosary faithfully:

> To all those who shall recite my rosary devoutly, I promise my special protection and very great graces.
>
> Those who shall persevere in the recitation of my rosary shall receive some signal grace.
>
> The rosary shall be a very powerful armor against hell; it will destroy vice, deliver from sin, and dispel heresy.
>
> The rosary will make virtue and good works flourish and will obtain for souls the most abundant divine mercies; it will substitute in

hearts love of God for love of the world, and it will lift them to the desire of heavenly and eternal things. How many souls shall sanctify themselves by this means!

Those who entrust themselves to me through the rosary shall not perish.

Those who shall recite my rosary devoutly, meditating on its mysteries, shall not be overwhelmed by misfortune. The sinner shall be converted; the just shall grow in grace and become worthy of eternal life.

Those truly devoted to my rosary shall not die without the sacraments of the Church.

Those who recite my rosary shall find during their life and at their death the light of God and the fullness of his graces and shall share in the merits of the blessed.

I shall deliver very promptly from purgatory the souls devoted to my rosary.

The true children of my rosary shall enjoy great glory in heaven.

What you ask through my rosary, you shall obtain.

Those who propagate my rosary shall be aided by me in all their necessities.

I have obtained from my son that all the members of the Rosary Confraternity shall have for their brethren the saints of heaven during their life and at the hour of death.

Those who recite my rosary faithfully are all my beloved children, the brothers and sisters of Jesus Christ.

Devotion to my rosary is a great sign of predestination.[35]

The rosary is a vocal sacramental. The prayers and the meditations on the life of Mary and Jesus, the mysteries, form a spiritual reminder of the Good News. As we pray, we imagine the scenes. We can see Jesus and Mary as they participate in God's plan of salvation, and we walk with them. The rosary engages our senses.

In the joyful mysteries of the rosary, Mary agrees to be the mother of Jesus. She travels to visit her cousin Elizabeth, who is carrying St. John in her womb. Mary gives birth. She brings her child to the temple in order to present him to God. Finally, she is relieved to find her twelve-year-old son after three days of searching. Jesus must be in his Father's house.

In his 2002 apostolic letter *Rosarium Virginis Mariae*, Pope John Paul II added the luminous mysteries of the rosary: Christ's baptism in the Jordan, the miracle at the wedding in Cana, the proclamation of the kingdom of God, the Transfiguration, and the institution of the Eucharist. The pope described each of these mysteries as "a revelation of the kingdom now present in the very person of Jesus."[36]

The sorrowful mysteries take us through the Lord's passion: his agony in the garden, scourging at the pillar, crowning with thorns, carrying of the cross, and death by crucifixion. "Here is found," the pope said, "*the culmination of the revelation of God's love* and the source of salvation."[37]

But "the contemplation of Christ's face cannot stop at the image of the Crucified One. He is the Risen One!"[38] Thus we have the glorious mysteries: the Resurrection, the Ascension, the descent of the Holy Spirit on the disciples, the assumption of the Blessed Mother into heaven, and her coronation as Queen of the Angels and Saints.

We pray to the Father, the Son, and the Holy Spirit as we begin the rosary with the Sign of the Cross. We hold the crucifix of the rosary, touching the image of the man who gave his life for us. We feel his sacrifice of love. And all he asks in return is our love.

We pray for the grace to love—to love our Father, Jesus, and the Holy Spirit, to love the Mother of God and our mother, to love one another.

::: **WITNESS** *(by Evelyn)* :::

When my husband, Gene, was young, he was told one year that the family could not have lights or ornaments for their Christmas tree. It was during the war, and there was nothing available, and evidently the ones from the previous year were not suitable.

That morning, Gene went on the bus with his mom to Mass. After Mass, he asked his mom for ten cents to light a candle in front of the Blessed Mother statue. He asked the Blessed Mother for ornaments and lights for their tree. They took the bus back home, and when they walked into the house, they found ornaments and lights all over the dining room table. The neighbor down the street had no children at home and thought the family would enjoy having the decorations. But Gene knew that the Blessed Mother had brought them to him. "She answered my prayer." From then on he had a special bond with Our Lady.

When Gene retired, he wanted to do something with no profit attached, and he decided to make rosaries. He got supplies, and he and his friend Sam started going to schools and talking about the rosary. Sam would pull out his rosary and say, "This is the best thing I have. She's my best friend. I always keep a rosary in my pocket." Gene and Sam would distribute rosaries in the school colors, four to five hundred at a time.

They sent ten thousand rosaries the color of sand to Iraq for our troops. They gave rosaries to nursing homes and veterans. Confirmation classes would ask for red rosaries, and RCIA classes, white ones.

Gene was a good man, and I feel the Blessed Mother herself probably welcomed him into heaven. After he died, I had a difficult time keeping up the rosary ministry but have done it by the grace of God.

I got a call last year for rosaries for the confirmation class at St. Henry and for a few for RCIA. I looked through our supply in the garage but could not find the red rosaries. The only ones I had were old and yellowed. So I went inside and said, "Blessed Mother, you've never failed me. Help me find those rosaries."

Determined, I went back to the garage, and I saw a bag marked "Purple and white, for Father Ryan High School." I thought, *Just check it anyway*, and sure enough, in the bottom of the bag, under the other rosaries, was a bag marked "St. Henry Confirmation." There were just enough red rosaries for the confirmation class and just enough white ones for the RCIA class. One more time, Our Lady came through for our family, just as she had for Gene the day he prayed for Christmas decorations.

::: GRACE :::

Mary wants us to come to her. She wants us to pray the rosary and to talk to her and ask her for all we need. Testaments of faith and love about the Virgin Mary are easy to come by because they are abundant. The more we spread the news of her goodness and her kindness, the more others will go to her.

Visit your mother in the rosary. She will fill you with her gifts of grace and peace. She loves us more than we could ever know.

A woman told me that she prays a family rosary. She names each of her family members on a bead. Then she moves on to the pope, her bishop, and priests.

I have started doing that myself. Our family is rather large, but I can still squeeze in the pope, the bishop, and a few priests each time. What a moment of grace to pray specifically for every member of my family each day—and for my family the Church!

::: PRAYER :::

Lord, your mother gave us the rosary to save us from the evil of this world. Help us to spread her devotion. Help us to honor her request that we pray the rosary. Help us meditate on your life and the grace of salvation you bring us.

::: **CHALLENGE** :::

Turn off the radio and the television, and pray the rosary.

::: CHAPTER TWENTY-THREE :::

Novenas

> When they had entered the city [of Jerusalem], they went to
> the room upstairs where they were staying. Peter, and John,
> and James, and Andrew, Philip and Thomas, Bartholomew
> and Matthew, James son of Alphaeus and Simon the Zealot,
> and Judas son of James. All these were constantly devoting
> themselves to prayer, together with certain women, including
> Mary the mother of Jesus, as well as his brothers.
>
> —Acts 1:13–14

A novena is a prayer said for nine days in thanksgiving and in petition
for a special intention. The word *novena* comes from the Latin word
novenus, which means "set of nine." In the early Church, novenas were
prayed during a nine-day mourning period for the repose of the soul of
a loved one. However, the first novena was the nine days following the
Ascension, when the apostles and Mary prayed in the Upper Room.
The novena ended on Pentecost Sunday, the time of the descent of
the Holy Spirit. Novenas are prayed to Jesus, Mary, the angels, and the
saints.

::: **WITNESS** *(by Jean)* :::

It's really difficult to share all that has happened through the years as
I have prayed novenas to St. Thérèse. I have received many roses in
answer to my prayer: a single random yellow rosebud lying across a
grave, a rose in full bloom on the bush at the bookstore in the dead of
winter, an unexpected delivery of roses, the air suddenly filled with the
fragrance of roses, the arrival of my granddaughter, Rose, and a visit
from Mama Rose, my mother-in-law.

Back when I was a freshman at St. Mary's Dominican and was worried that my daddy was not going to Mass, I prayed the Christmas Novena. Daddy was the most positive influence in my life, often sitting at the kitchen table reading the Bible. But he just wouldn't go to Mass unless he looked like a million dollars, with nice shoes and clothes. During the time I was praying the novena, he made his confession and went back to church.

When I say a novena, that keeps the prayer going solid for that length of time. When the woman in the Gospel finally went to Jesus for healing, the physical touch of Jesus's cloak, along with her faith and her prayer, allowed Jesus to heal her (see Mark 5:25–34). When we give Jesus something to work with, like nine days of prayer, he answers us. Maybe not right away, and only if it's a good thing, but he answers.

Sometimes too, the answer may not be a direct one, but let's give credit to God for guiding the doctors who find cures for the problems we have with our physical selves. Let's thank God for sending us the communion of saints, who help us in our times of need and fear and desire.

::: **GRACE** :::

Novena prayers are great sacramentals to pass along to friends and family. They are usually printed in pamphlets or on cards, so they are easy to pass around. My mom used to tape all sorts of things to the bathroom mirrors. I thank God for her passing along her devotion to novenas.

One Sunday a friend who is a nurse came up to me after Mass and shared her success story of praying the novena to St. Thérèse. "I had prayed the novena of St. Thérèse and had not received any confirmation, so to speak. You know, a rose of some sort or the scent of roses. I guessed my need would go unanswered or the timing of my request was just not God's time. Then, the next week, I was assigned to be your grandmother Rose's nurse. I got my Rose! I knew that my prayer request had been heard and one way or the other, all would be well." I loved to hear the story of the novena in another's life just as I had heard so many times from my mother.

One year I gave out the St. Andrew Christmas Novena to a mothers' group after giving a little talk and sharing some Christmas traditions. Most of the women had never heard of this devotion, but I had seen prayers answered through it and wanted to spread it around every chance I got. Months later, one of my friends caught me after Mass and said, "Hey, I want to thank you. My wife and I had been trying to have another child with no success. We did the Christmas Novena together and have recently found out we are going to have another baby."

"Well, hey," I responded. "That's not me. That's the power of prayer. Thank God for that."

Novena to St. Thérèse of the Child Jesus

St. Thérèse, the Little Flower of Jesus,
please pick a rose from the heavenly garden,
and send it to me with a message of love.
I ask you to obtain for me the favors that I seek:
(Here mention your request.)
Recommend my request to Mary, Queen of Heaven,
so that she may intercede for me, with you, before her Son,
Jesus Christ.
If this favor is granted, I will love you more and more and be
better prepared to spend eternal happiness with you in heaven.
St. Thérèse of the Little Flower, pray for me.[39]

Christmas Novena

Say this prayer fifteen times a day from St. Andrew's Day, November 30, until Christmas:

Hail, and blessed be the hour and moment
At which the Son of God was born
Of a most pure Virgin
At a stable at midnight in Bethlehem
In the piercing cold.
At that hour vouchsafe, I beseech Thee,
To hear my prayers and grant my desires *(mention request here)*.
Through Jesus Christ and his most Blessed Mother.[40]

Oftentimes, we are too busy to pray, or so we think. But when we take the time to pray, God often makes more time available for us. And we are filled with what we really need: gifts of grace. Time in prayer is time well spent.

Learning the prayer stories of those steeped in the love of Christ is a true blessing. We become Christ to one another.

::: PRAYER :::

Lord, help me to use the prayers given by Jesus and Mary and the saints of the Church for the intentions of others. I pray for those in need, as I know others pray for me.

May the rhythm of repetitive prayers help me focus on your love for people in need and your power to help them. And may my prayers and desires be conformed to your holy will.

::: CHALLENGE :::

Pray a nine-day novena for a person close to your heart.

CHAPTER TWENTY-FOUR

Chaplets

> The chaplets are crowns which we can use to bring greater honor and glory to Our Lord, his Blessed Mother, the angels and the saints. They also are forming crowns for our own heavenly glory, by storing our treasures in heaven.[41]
>
> —PATRICIA QUINTILIAN, *MY TREASURY OF CHAPLETS*

A chaplet is prayed on a set of beads, much like a rosary. The prayers said on the beads are prayers of devotion to Jesus, Mary, or one of the saints. We can pray a chaplet for a specific need or simply to honor an aspect of the life of a holy one. The beads help us in our meditation and remind us to constantly pray to Jesus and Mary and the other holy men and women in heaven.

There are many popular chaplets. The Chaplet of Divine Mercy is a prayer for mercy to Jesus Christ, our pure example of love and forgiveness. It calls us to trust in him over all that the world has to offer us. There are other chaplets that honor God and Mary, such as the Chaplet of the Infant of Prague, the Chaplet of the Five Wounds, the Chaplet of the Sacred Heart, the Chaplet of the Seven Sorrows and the Seven Joys, and the Chaplet of the Holy Spirit.

The St. Michael Chaplet requests protection in the day-to-day battle with the ways of the outside world, the flesh, and the devil. Many other saints have chaplets, which we pray to honor them but also for specific intentions. We might pray St. Thérèse's Chaplet to help us live more simply, as she taught with her Little Way. St. Jude is ready to help us for what might seem impossible. St. Anne, the mother of Mary, is a good saint to ask for a favor involving parenting. St. Peregrine is a patron for people diagnosed with cancer.

The Chaplet of Divine Mercy

St. Maria Faustina was a sister in the Congregation of Sisters of Our Lady of Mercy in Krakow, Poland. Like many other saints we read about, she had the humblest jobs in the kitchen, in the garden, and as a doorkeeper in the convent.

On February 22, 1931, Jesus appeared to Sr. Faustina with a message of mercy. He was dressed in a white garment, with one hand raised in blessing and the other touching the garment at the breast. Two rays, one red and one white, came forth from his breast. Jesus asked Sr. Maria Faustina to have this image painted, with the inscription beneath, "Jesus, I Trust in You."

In 1934, Sr. Faustina began keeping a personal diary, which today gives the whole world access to Jesus's messages of mercy. In 1935, Jesus gave Sr. Faustina the Chaplet of Divine Mercy, which can be prayed on regular rosary beads:

> You will recite it for nine days, on the beads of the rosary, in the following manner: First of all, you will say one Our Father and Hail Mary and the I Believe in God. Then on the Our Father beads you will say the following words: "Eternal Father, I offer You the Body and Blood, Soul and Divinity of Your dearly beloved Son, Our Lord Jesus Christ, in atonement for our sins and those of the whole world." On the Hail Mary beads, you will say the following words: "For the sake of His sorrowful Passion, have mercy on us and on the whole world." In conclusion, three times you will recite these words: "Holy God, Holy Mighty One, Holy Immortal One, have mercy on us and on the whole world."[42]

::: **WITNESS** *(by Father John)* :::

Pope John Paul II made the second Sunday of Easter Divine Mercy Sunday for the whole Church. That means that the Divine Mercy is for the whole parish.

After the homily at all the Masses on this Sunday, I have everyone come up and venerate the Divine Mercy image, as St. Faustina requested. During the time the people are venerating, I read passages from St. Faustina's *Diary*. Just as ashes and palms, which are sacramentals, are brought into the sacred liturgy at the appropriate times, so too the Divine Mercy is brought into the Mass. Hopefully more parishes will realize and celebrate fully Divine Mercy Sunday.

Our parish also promotes the Divine Mercy Novena. I encourage families and individuals to pray privately. This in turn enables them to really pray the public sacred liturgy.

::: **GRACE** :::

Learning the intense devotion of others in our community gives us examples to follow. It can fill us with the desire to go and do the same.

My friend, Jack, shared with me his promotion of the *Diary* of St. Faustina and the Chaplet of Divine Mercy. I could not write fast enough to keep up with the experiences and the graces he recounted. He has given out thousands of novena booklets and pamphlets and has spent countless hours praying in jails and nursing homes as well as with the dying. He promotes the Divine Mercy because he wants all to experience the gift Christ promises. The Lord told St. Faustina:

> It pleases me to grant everything souls ask of me by saying the chaplet. When hardened sinners say it, I will fill their souls with peace, and the hour of their death will be a happy one.

Write this for the benefit of distressed souls; when a soul sees and realizes the gravity of its sins, when the whole abyss of the misery into which it immersed itself is displayed before its eyes, let it not despair, but with trust let it throw itself into the arms of My mercy, as a child into the arms of its beloved mother. Tell them no soul that has called upon My mercy has been disappointed or brought to shame. I delight particularly in a soul that has placed its trust in My goodness. Write that when they say this Chaplet in the presence of the dying, I will stand between My Father and the dying person, not as the Just Judge but as the Merciful Saviour.[43]

::: PRAYER :::

Lord, you graciously give us these gifts of prayer for our specific needs and desires. Help us to pray for ourselves and others, especially those who are imprisoned, sick, or dying. May our prayers rise up for those who cannot pray for themselves. Have mercy on us and on the whole world.

::: CHALLENGE :::

Obtain and pray a chaplet. If you know someone who is dying, pray specifically the Chaplet of Divine Mercy for that person.

::: CONCLUSION :::

Grace is the favor, the free and undeserved help that God gives us to respond to his call to become children of God, adoptive sons, partakers of the divine nature and of eternal life. Grace is a participation in the life of God.

—*CATECHISM OF THE CATHOLIC CHURCH,* 1996, 1997

I know how easy it is to belong to an organization, a committee, or an association. All I have to do is sign up and attend some meetings. But all of us know that to receive the "good parts" of anything, we need to participate. We need to engage in all that is offered and make the most of the benefits. Why join and just sit there?

The Catholic Church is filled with rich benefits that can bring us closer to God, and sacramentals are some of the benefits she has to offer. When we faithfully and prayerfully engage in using sacramentals, we receive favor from God. We experience the grace that enables us to participate more fully in the life of the Church and to gain help for our day from God.

As I read Jason Evert's *Saint John Paul the Great: His Five Loves,* I was particularly moved by the Pope's lifelong use of sacramentals.

At six in the morning, at noon, and again at six in the evening, he would stop whatever he was doing to pray the Angelus, just as he had done while working in the chemical plant in Poland. He prayed several rosaries each day, went to confession every week, and did not let a day pass without receiving Holy Communion. Each Friday (and every Lent) he prayed the Stations of the Cross, and preferred to do this in the garden on the roof of the Papal Apartments. During Lent, he would eat one complete meal a day, and always fasted on the eve of

Our Lady's feast days. He remarked, "If the bishop doesn't set an example by fasting, then who will?" The Holy Father knew that his first duty to the Church was his interior life.[44]

These sacramentals of the Church, used by the pope daily, sustained him. They became a natural part of his life. And the more we use these gifts from the Church that help to lead us into favor with God, the more they will become the same for us—a natural part of our lives.

Through the prayerful use of sacramentals, we are drawn closer to Christ. As we participate more fully in the riches of our faith, we reap the benefits; we receive the gifts that God wants us to have to live more deeply in his love. As we have already said, there is no magic to sacramentals, and we certainly do not need them for salvation. But I think that putting more thought and prayer to what we already do, such as signing ourselves, or adding one of the many other sacramentals to our daily or weekly routines, can certainly bring us closer to the sacraments and to a greater participation in the life of God.

::: ACKNOWLEDGMENTS :::

The Witness portions of this book were contributed by many dear friends and people of faith. Special thanks goes to:

- Mary Ann Beavin, St. Matthew School, Franklin, Tennessee
- Deacon Joe Holzmer, Cathedral of the Incarnation, Nashville, Tennessee
- Catherine Birdwell, Holy Family Parish, Brentwood, Tennessee
- John Murphree, St. Henry Church, Nashville, Tennessee
- Sarah Knies, St. Henry Church, Nashville, Tennessee
- Sr. Mary Angela, Dominican Sisters of St. Cecilia, Nashville, Tennessee
- Mary Forte Campbell, St. Ann Church, Nashville, Tennessee
- Jim Bauchiero, St. Matthew Church, Franklin, Tennessee
- Philip Alexander, St. Henry Parish, Nashville, Tennessee
- Sr. Clare Therese, Dominican Sisters of St. Cecilia, Nashville, Tennessee
- Evelyn Mulloy, St. Henry Church, Nashville, Tennessee
- Fr. John Kirk, Pastor of Church of the Nativity, Spring Hill, Tennessee
- Jean Dortch, my mom

::: NOTES :::

1. Pope Francis, Vigil of Pentecost with the Ecclesial Movements, May 18, 2013, transcript and link to video by Vatican Radio, Libreria Editrice Vaticana, http://w2.vatican.va/content/francesco/en/speeches/2013/may/documents/papa-francesco_20130518_veglia-pentecoste.html.

2. Tertullian, *De Corona*, chap. 3, in Alexander Roberts and James Donaldson, ed., *The Ante-Nicene Fathers*, vol. 3 (Peabody, Mass.: Hendrickson, 2004), p. 94.

3. St. Cyril of Jerusalem, *Catecheses* xiii, 36, in Leo P. McCauley, S.J., and Anthony A. Stephenson, trans., *The Fathers of the Church*, vol. 2 (Washington, D.C.: Catholic University Press, 1970), p. 28.

4. Excerpt from the *Lectionary for Mass for Use in the Dioceses of the United States of America*, 2nd ed., 2001, Confraternity of Christian Doctrine, Inc., Washington, D.C.

5. Letter of St. Pope John Paul II to Bishop Albert Houssiau of Liège, on the occasion of the 750th anniversary of the Feast of the Body of Christ, quoting *Lumen Gentium*, 28.

6. St. Alphonsus Liguori, "Quotes on the Most Blessed Sacrament, 15," Real Presence Eucharistic Education and Adoration Association, http://www.therealpresence.org/eucharst/tes/quotes15.html.

7. Code of Canon Law, 942 (Canon Law Society, 1983).

8. Mother Teresa of Calcutta, as quoted in Lavonne Neff, *A Life for God: The Mother Teresa Reader* (Ann Arbor, Mich.: Charis, 1995), p. 188.

9. *General Instruction of the Roman Missal*, Vatican, http://www. vatican.va/roman_curia/congregations/ccdds/documents/rc_con_ ccdds_doc_20030317_ordinamento-messale_en.html#C._The_ Liturgy_of_the_Eucharist.

10. St. Francis de Sales, *Introduction to the Devout Life*, trans., ed., and intro. John K. Ryan, bk. 3, chap. 23 (New York: Image, 2003), pp. 172–173.

11. St. Alphonsus Liguori, *The Way of the Cross* (Baltimore: Barton Cotton, 1977), foreword.

12. *The Enchiridion of Indulgences Norms and Grants*, authorized English ed. (n.p.: Sacred Apostolic Penitentiary, 1968), no. 63, p. 74.

13. St. John Vianney, Sermon 7, *Sermons of the Curé d'Ars* (Charlotte, N.C.: Tan, 1995), p. 230.

14. Tertullian, *Apology*, chap.16.

15. Thomas à Kempis, *The Imitation of Christ*, (New York: Confraternity of the Precious Blood, 1954, bk. 2, chap. 12, p. 145.

16. United States Conference of Catholic Bishops, *Built of Living Stones: Art, Architecture, and Worship* (Washington, D.C.: USCCB, 2005), no. 91, p. 34.

17. Prayer before a Crucifix, *The Catholic Source Book* (Huntington, Ind.: Our Sunday Visitor, 2008), p. 13.

18. *The General Instruction of the Roman Missal*, no. 150 (Washington, D.C.: United States Conference of Catholic Bishops, 2011), p. 55.

19. "The Oil of Saint Philomena," Sanctuary of Saint Philomena, para. 4, http://www.philomena.us/about-the-sanctuary/ oil-saint-philomena/.

20. "On Certain Questions Regarding the Collaboration of the Non-Ordained Faithful in the Sacred Ministry of Priest," Libreria Editrice Vaticana, http://www.vatican.va/roman_curia/pontifical_councils/laity/documents/rc_con_interdic_doc_15081997_en.html.

21. National Shrine of the Infant Jesus of Prague, Prague, Oklahoma, "History of the Miraculous Infant Jesus of Prague," www.shrineofinfantjesus.com/IJhistory.

22. "Infant of Prague Novena Prayer," Eternal Word Television Network, http://www.ewtn.com/library/PRAYER/PRAGNOV.TXT.

23. Donna-Marie Cooper O'Boyle, *The Miraculous Medal: Stories, Prayers and Devotions* (Cincinnati: Servant, 2013), p. x.

24. "The Medal of St. Benedict," Order of St. Benedict, www.osb.org. Link for page referenced? http://www.osb.org/gen/medal.html

25. Fr. John Croiset, S.J., *The Devotion to the Sacred Heart of Jesus* (Charlotte, N.C.: Tan, 2007), p. 91.

26. *Catholic Source Book*, p. 358.

27. Sacred Heart Badge Card, Our Lady of the Rosary Library, http://www.olrl.org/pray/shbadge_card.shtml.

28. *The Pieta Prayer Book*, (Hickory Corners, Mich.: Miraculous Lady of the Roses, 2004).

29. Catherine Doherty, *Strannik: The Call to the Pilgrimage of the Heart* (Combermere, Ont.: Madonna House, 2012), p. 47.

30. Catherine and Peter Fournier, Marian Devotion in the Domestic Church (San Francisco: Ignatius, 2007) p. 30.

31. St. Jerome, *Ad Riparium*, I, P.L., XXII, 907, in Philip Schaff, D.D.LL., and Henry Wace, eds., *Nicene and Post-Nicene Fathers*, vol. 6 (Peabody, Mass.: Hendrickson, 2004), p. 212.

32. *Catholic Source Book*, p. 351, citing Second Council of Nicaea.

33. "Brown Scapular or Scapular of Our Lady of Mount Carmel," Eternal Television Network, http://www.ewtn.com/expert/ answers/brown_scapular.HTM.

34. *Rosarium Virginis Mariae*, 3.

35. "Fifteen Promises of Our Lady," *The Original Pieta Prayer Book* (Hickory Corners, Mich.: Miraculous Lady of the Roses, 1972).

36. *Rosarium Virginis Mariae*, 21.

37. *Rosarium Virginis Mariae*, 22. Emphasis in original.

38. *Rosarium Virginis Mariae*, quoting *Novo Millennio Ineunte*, 29.

39. Rev. Victor Hoagland, C.P., ed., *Manual of Catholic Devotions* (Melville, N.Y.: Regina, 2003), pp. 132–133.

40. "Christmas Novena," Eternal Television Network, https://www. ewtn.com/Devotionals/novena/christmas.htm.

41. Patricia S. Quintiliani, *My Treasury of Chaplets* (Still River, Mass.: Ravengate, 2006), p. xiii.

42. Maria Faustina Kowalska, *Diary of Saint Maria Faustina Kowalska: Divine Mercy in My Soul* (Stockbridge, Mass.: Marian, 2013), p. 208.

43. Kowalska, pp. 547–548.

44. Jason Evert, *Saint John Paul the Great* (Lakeland, Colo.: Totus Tuus, 2014), pp. 128–129.

ABOUT THE AUTHOR

Julie Cragon and her husband, Allen, have six children and co-own St. Mary's Bookstore and Church Supply with her mother, Jean Dortch, and her sister, Donna Turner. She is a native of Nashville, Tennessee and graduated from Vanderbilt University. Julie is the author of *Bless My Child, Jesus at My Side,* and *Visiting Mary: Her U.S. Shrines and Their Graces.* She has worked on many gift book projects including the *Illustrated Book of Mary,* the *Illustrated Book of Jesus,* and the *Illustrated Lives of the Saints* both for adults and children. She is one of the founding members of the Catholic Retailers Association.